Fasting is Not About Food

By

Heather Eschenbaum

Dedicated to the heroes
of my life...
my husband and my father, both
named John.
My life has forever been
transformed by
your love.

TABLE OF CONTENTS

My Thanksgiving Misfortune

Food is *everywhere*! Every party you attend and every holiday your family shares is centered around food. Grocery stores, restaurants and even gas stations are full of specialty food and desserts. Advertisements bombard your senses! Overwhelming aromas assault you as you drive down the street. Co-workers bring scrumptious donuts to work and people suddenly act like they haven't eaten in years! In our culture, most people don't go more than three hours without food. And many people have never fasted in their lives. Whether we are celebrating life or honoring a person in death, we surround ourselves with food.

While every single holiday or family

gathering is about food, Thanksgiving is no exception. This holiday is like the Championship of Food Consumption! It's a time that everyone in America can eat until they no longer feel their legs. It's not only acceptable to gorge yourself, but completely expected. To think of not having the entire buffet including turkey, stuffing, gravy, mashed potatoes, rolls and Aunt Betty's famous pumpkin pie would be sacrilegious to most Americans. No one would consider fasting through such a monumental day; unless that someone decided to do a twenty-one day fast and didn't consult the calendar when starting it two weeks before Thanksgiving.

Yes, I did the unthinkable. I started a twenty-one day fast and didn't realize Thanksgiving was in the last week! As soon as it became clear what I had done, I began the negotiations in my mind. Maybe cranberry sauce and mashed potatoes would be acceptable. Oh, and gravy is liquid… so that should be okay. Maybe I could eat that day and be exonerated since it was a holiday. Holiday food doesn't count against a fast, right? At this point, many of you would have thrown in the towel and heartily welcomed the feast that was coming. Maybe you hadn't heard right when you felt the Lord calling you to fast. Surely Thanksgiving is one of the biblical feasts! The Lord could've been confused when He called you to fast through it.

After all of my negotiations and a short period of mourning, I finally decided it was was best to fast through Thanksgiving. But that's crazy! Who fasts through Thanksgiving? *I must not be an American.*

Hope and young dedication propelled me into fasting through a Thanksgiving I will never forget. My initial thought was that I could lock myself away from the aromas wafting through, saturating every room of the house. And when I say *'lock myself away'* I mean, *'find a dungeon and lock myself in some medieval arm and leg shackles, and build a moat around me.'* Unfortunately, that wouldn't be the case because my little, farmer Grandfather would be coming. He was a bit senile and I knew he wouldn't understand why I wasn't at the dinner table. Even if I tried to explain what fasting was and why I was doing it, I knew he couldn't fathom it... heck, you don't have to be senile to think it's crazy to fast during Thanksgiving.

"Hope and young dedication propelled me into fasting through a Thanksgiving I will never forget."

As I catered to my Grandfather, I not only showed up for dinner, I helped make it. I was in charge of the mashed potatoes - the glorious, magnificent mashed potatoes. Encompassing smells and sights were abounding that day as we worked in the kitchen bringing forth a delectable feast. But boy, those potatoes were messy. Multiple times as I mashed, gooey potato would end up on my finger and I would cringe inwardly as I wiped it on the towel. I can still picture that towel so vividly in my mind! It was green and white plaid, in case you were wondering. I haven't been a big fan of green plaid since then.

As we sat down to the spread, I was seated between my husband and my Grandfather. As food was passed around to me, I took a small portion of each and placed it on my beautiful, white and gold china. I was thankful that my Grandfather was senile, and he didn't notice that for the next half hour I was swirling and circulating the food around my plate. I can still recall the colors mixing together. I essentially played with my food as my insides cried out to eat. Multiple times I snuck a few pieces over to my husband's plate.

Just when I took a sigh of relief that I made it through dinner, they brought out the desserts! *'Well, I can't stop the charades now. Give me a sliver of everything!'* I swirled the pies around until I almost made a sugary soup. Believe me, it didn't get better later in the day. That's when everyone comes out of their food coma to have seconds and thirds. Thanksgiving is an ongoing torture chamber for a faster. Believe me, I know. My mother had such compassion for me and promised to freeze my favorites. But, nothing tastes as good when it's thawed out. Nothing.

Looking back on that day, I know my heart wanted to do whatever it took to reach God. I believed that fasting was the ticket to be closer to Him and to becoming the young woman I'd always hoped to become. God honored my attempt, and I continued to pursue. But I knew that what I read in the Bible didn't match up with what I was experiencing. I was missing something.

Hello. My name is Heather and I'm an expert at fasting. Well, at the very least, I'm an expert at fasting the wrong way. To truly be an expert, I believe a person must not only be knowledgable on how to do something, but more importantly, he or she must know how *not* to do something. And when it comes to fasting, most people fail before they even begin. My guess is that you've failed at fasting a few times yourself, and maybe consider yourself an expert at fasting the wrong way, otherwise you wouldn't be picking up this book.

Aren't you tired of failing at fasting? Join me on this journey as I show you the truth... that *fasting is not about food.*

You Might Be Fasting Wrong If...

The world is full of people who go to great lengths to starve themselves and deny their bodies of food, but they feel they're missing something... something other than the double cheeseburger they're craving. Before I get ahead of myself and teach on fasting, let me cover some of the basics of how *not* to fast. I'm sure you will see yourself in many of these epic fails. Sadly, I can write about them so well because I've lived through most of them on more than one occasion! So let's get started:

- **Irrational Hunger.** Ever notice how you aren't necessarily hungry until someone asks you to join them in a fast? You could've just waddled slowly out of a buffet restaurant as your friend casually says, *'You know, we really ought to pray and fast for our nation starting today.'* Suddenly you are imagining life without food and you shudder at the thought. Maybe you should've had that third dessert plate and stocked up like a camel for what was to come.

- **Purging.** The night before starting a fast, the *'Garfield Syndrome'* comes on you. Remember how he threw back his head and gobbled up the lasagna? Yes, that is how you look. Everything in the fridge, freezer and pantry ends up being scarfed down in order to free the house from temptation. It's a type of deep cleansing to prevent the pull from any decadent, rich, yummy goodness calling out to you as you start your fast the following day. I know I'm not the only one who has actually gained weight on a fast as I purged the house and then lost the willpower to start the fast the next day. I still remember a half-gallon of Rocky Road ice cream that I needed to 'remove' before I started my twenty-one day fast the following Monday. Coincidentally, I don't remember the fast or if I even started it, but I still remember that ice cream! And how does the house always fill up with an abundance of food before you decide you have been called to fast again? Unfortunately, you never think to fast when your shelves and fridge are bare.

- **Food Channels.** During the first few days of fasting, you become the most dedicated fan of the food channels. Not only do you know every show and chef, but you might've ordered multiple cookbooks and even made some of the food as a sacrifice to your family. Ironically, my husband has eaten some of the best meals of his life while I was fasting. I was careful, however, not to let one bite pass my lips even as I cooked that succulent meal with great love and care.

- **Infomercials.** Every blender, cooker, cutter, steamer and juicer seems to be sold with great fervency in those pre-dawn hours. It is like the TV networks are targeting

insomniacs, drunks and fasting zombies...
people in some of the most vulnerable
moments of their lives! Infomercials are like
the food channel on drugs. These shows
make you ravenous even when you aren't
fasting. You shouldn't watch them when
you are fasting and in such a feeble state of
mind and body.

- **Overeating.** Even though I was 'fasting,'
many times I remember wolfing down
gigantic amounts of fruits and vegetables.
If eating a watermelon the size of a toddler
is considered your morning snack, you
probably aren't fasting. And if you are
setting up a buffet of every fruit and
vegetable known to man or juicing twenty-
seven times a day, it probably isn't a
spiritual fast. You can't be focused on God
much if you are constantly cleaning your
juicer of pulp or cutting up the next fruit
and veggie buffet.

- **Cough Drops.** While fasting, you might not
feel your best. A possible cold might be
coming on! Time to buy a plethora of

sugary goodness in the form of a cough drop. It's for your health, right?

- **Toothpaste.** Many fasters love to brush their teeth multiple times a day to get a sugar fix. While fasting, toothpaste begins to taste like mint ice cream. I know I've had some of the cleanest teeth ever during my longer fasts.

- **Dessert-Flavored Gum.** These flavors were without a doubt invented for fasters. During the fast, you may not be eating any food, but you can have your favorite pie-flavored gum swirling around your tongue as you chomp. You're like a smoker. Just ask any faster, *'How many packs a day do you chew on a fast?'* Their response will naturally be, *'Well, I'm up to two packs a day, but I can stop anytime, especially once I get to eat again.'*

- **Legal Liquids.** Many people say that if it's in liquid form, then you're still fasting. I have a friend who confessed to me that while fasting she would take small chocolates and let them melt in her mouth until they were 'liquid and legal.' Heck if you are gonna do that, then you should melt a dozen in the microwave and drink those babies down!

- **Condiments.** When fasting, you become a sauce connoisseur. Surely, all dressings are permissible. No need to check the ingredients, right? Sauces and dressings can become a very slippery slope, my friend. For those of you who have done a Daniel Fast, you know what I mean. Suddenly, dressing is a staple of life as you try to munch down all of the new, healthy salads and vegetables that you wouldn't imagine eating before. And please don't think of taking away people's beloved ketchup or mayo. You've got to have those for the veggie french fries!

- **Negotiations.** Debates begin quickly as you search through your cookbooks. Everything starts to look like a fruit or vegetable. Surely french fries and a strawberry shake from the Drive-Thru are acceptable on a Daniel Fast! The main ingredients are strawberries and potatoes for goodness sake! One time while on a Daniel Fast, I was at a restaurant and ate some grilled mushrooms that had been cooked near the steaks. I immediately ordered more: *'Please send me an entire platter of those steaks... er... I mean... mushrooms!'* At any point in a fast, anything you eat will be scrumptious. Even an old, dried out fruitcake from two Christmases ago would taste good. Fruit is in the name, people! Surely you should eat that and make your Grandma proud.

• **Food Dreams.** Every faster has experienced this — constant food dreams that usually include buffets or pizza! If your days are filled with cookbooks, recipes, food discussions and aching for food, then your dreams will be filled with... you guessed it, food. These dreams cause a roller-coaster of emotion as you're ecstatic to be eating again, but you're overcome with tremendous guilt when you wake up.

These highs and lows of fasting can be excruciating.

- **Water Dreams.** If you are doing a complete fast, having neither food nor water, you'll dream of only water. After the first day, food will not be an issue. Water will be your only focus. You'll daydream of waterfalls, rivers, and penny fountains at the mall... glorious, beautiful water gushing everywhere you look. And whatever you do, don't get caught out in a rainstorm. Pure torture. It's like chocolate raindrops pouring down on your body as they fall from the sky and you can't lick off a single one. I did a fast like this once. Once was all I needed, to know I would never do it again. Ever watch a rescue story about how someone was trapped in a cave and drank every liquid imaginable to stay alive? When hearing stories like that I often wondered, *'How on earth could they drink that?'* Well, do a complete fast and you will understand. Water was all I could think about. I would have drunk water from flower vases, dirty puddles and seriously considered toilet water after two days.

- **The Scale.** Many people see the fast as a last ditch effort to lose weight. If you're fasting for your health, that is one thing. But if you're spiritually fasting, the scale should not be your focus. Unfortunately, as I was fasting, I would visit the scale more often than I'd like to admit. I don't remember that being part of Esther's story. I can't imagine her standing around the scale with her handmaidens and saying, *'Whew! This fasting thing is really paying off! I look amazing! Thanks, Mordecai!'*

- **The Refrigerator.** For some, the scale is your BFF; for others, it is the fridge. You know you shouldn't be sulking around the kitchen, but that doesn't stop you. Somehow there's a fierce magnetism between you and that portion of your house. It's a stronger gravitational pull than standing next to a black hole. Many times while fasting, you might have found yourself gazing into the lighted plethora of food, hearing angelic songs, while knowing you aren't supposed to be eating anything from it. I've even decided to clean the fridge while fasting. Surely it's as good of a time as any to throw out that expired food, making myself useful as I stand in awe of the fridge's contents. Then I can freeze anything that might go bad before I get the chance to eat it, right? Multi-tasking at its finest.

- **Accidental Eating.** I can't count the times I've forgotten I was fasting and taken a bite of something scrumptious. As you accidentally taste the food, you never think, *'Oops! I'm fasting; I'll just set the rest of that down and go back to prayer.'* No, you take a bite and think, *'Oh no! I'm fasting! I can't recover from this! I might as well start stuffing my face with the entire fridge.'* Whatever was accidentally bitten into will be devoured in seconds.

- **Communion.** Taking outrageous amounts of communion while on a fast is not considered fasting. Instead of the small morsel that you receive at church, you are downing a gallon of grape juice and the largest loaf of 'spiritual' bread you can find at the store. While fasting in my early days, I couldn't be trusted to have juice and bread in the house, let alone take a small nibble of it and leave the rest!

- **Anger.** Everyone fears the rage that can come out of a person who is fasting. Even the kindest, old missionary lady can turn into a raving maniac if you don't give her her coffee and chocolate. *Hint: If you are more angry, selfish or bitter as you fast, you're doing it wrong.* And I beg you to stop, at least for the sake of your family, especially the children! Fasting will teach you so much about yourself. You don't need to go to any seminar to understand the depths of your psyche. Just tell your flesh that it isn't getting any food for twenty-one days and there will be a meltdown.

- **Electronics.** Instead of increasing your prayers and Bible study during the fast, you're glued to electronics of all kinds. While fasting, it seems that everyone is eating on every single TV show or movie. Instead of setting aside time to fast and pray, we try to fill our every waking thought to keep from gorging ourselves. The problem is that the TV only feeds your addiction to eat. It makes you hungry even when you're not fasting!

- **Stopwatch Fasting.** For many fasters, the clock brings failure or success. I believed there was a countdown that I had to follow instead of following the Spirit. If I started a three day fast and ended it a few hours before the full three days, then I believed it couldn't count at all. That way of thinking says anytime I make a mistake, it renders all of my previous good work null and void.

On the flip side, I heard of a family that would end their fast at midnight with a massive barbecue. Interestingly, they would start the prep for the meal at 9 p.m. so they could eat the surplus of food at the exact stroke of midnight. If your thoughts and hands are filled with food, are you really fasting at all?

- **Buffet Finish.** Even if you have fasted flawlessly, ending a fast is where most people fall off the deep end. In your mind you're sure you'll have great self-control as you start with an orange or even an apple. But as you bite into that succulent fruit, your mind and body become crazed with food lust. Your tastebuds are awakened with a passion you've never felt before. Nothing will stop you now. First the orange, then immediately a steak, then a cheeseburger, then ice cream and so on. Your orange has now turned into a fifteen-course smorgasbord, making up swiftly for all the meals you lost.

While writing this chapter, I laughed so hard I cried. The words flowed way too smoothly. Great humor is found in all of these examples because they are too true. While we all hope to be strong men and women of God, we must realize how easily our unbiblical beliefs about fasting and prayer knock us out before we even begin.

I'm sure that many of you have your own stories and that you could relate to many of these epic fails. But don't give up! Keep reading and I promise you will find new hope and freedom as we continue on...

Humble Beginnings

Let's be honest, most people don't know how to fast and pray. They've never truly lived a life of empowered, biblical fasting and prayer... and I was one of them.

My decision to try spiritual fasting was birthed out of a desire to be closer to God. All my life I was told God was real, but I hadn't experienced Him like I had read about in the Bible. Without training and time to grow in my relationship with God, I believed that fasting was the ticket not only to get me closer to Him, but to prove that I was serious about my relationship with Him. I attempted every type of fasting: juicing, water only, fruits and vegetables, and so on. My desire to know Him was so strong and heartfelt, but I had limited training and understanding about fasting and prayer.

Every day I meet people just like this —
Christians struggling in their relationship, even as
they are wanting to do the very best in their walk
with God. As these people tell me that they've
been called by God to fast, I ask them a simple
question: *'What else has God told you to do?'* Most
cannot give me an answer. As Christians, many
believe the only thing God has ever called them
to do is fast, taking away their food.

How sad it must be to God, that fasting has
been twisted to such a great degree, that we
immediately identify it with taking things away
from His sons and daughters. This is a
conundrum to me. Who wants to be in a
relationship with someone who says the same
exact thing every single day? Even if my husband
was telling me how amazingly gorgeous I was
and nothing else, it would get very old by the
second day; well, at least by the third day. And
how many of you would last in a relationship
where the other person told you fasting was the
only way to get closer to them and said nothing
else? The funny thing is, if I thought that starving
myself would cause my husband to love me

more, we probably wouldn't be married!

I know that our God asks more of us than to fast, but Christians all around the world believe this is the answer. They start with such zeal and excitement as they prepare and feel called to a twenty-one day fast, but by the end of day one they are found clutching a donut box, mumbling words of regret.

I propose that there are times that Christians are not called to fast like they believe. But instead, the devil knows how much you fail and calls you to another '*spiritual fast*' to cause you to lose heart and pull you away from God. I know this might be difficult for some to comprehend, but the enemy will tell you to do '*spiritual things*' in a ploy to cause failure and ultimately separation from God. *Sometimes we must realize that we have put God in a position where He looks much more like an abuser, instead of the Father He truly is.*

Remember, we are spiritual beings, with angelic and demonic activity constantly going on above us. You need to be discerning and realize not everything you hear comes from God. Your job is to develop your relationship with the Lord, which in turn will cause you to know His voice. Without relationship, you will listen to anything crossing your path and the enemy will take full advantage of that. *Satan will manipulate you, but God will train you.* And your enemy knows there is no greater way to trip up your growth than to hear your enemy speak spiritual things that seem right, but push you further away from your Father.

As a parent, you would never ask your child to do something you knew he failed at over and over again. You'd never expect your toddler to run a marathon. Every family member is ecstatic when they see their child attempt to take their first steps. With those steps, there are always exuberant celebrations and loads of pictures. No mother would be heard saying, *'Now, Tommy, I expected so much more from you! Get back up and run around the room thirty times. This falling down is unacceptable.'* Our God is excited for us to take a single step. And every step gets us closer to walking with Him.

Sadly, I am surprised and saddened at how many unseasoned, baby Christians shun the idea of fasting one meal as they embark on a forty day water fast, believing it will cause them to truly reach God. The *quality* of the fast is much more important and life-changing than the longevity of it. Quality is paramount. I could fast one meal and watch God move more powerfully in my life than most do in forty days. Why? Because of relationship. *I fast out of relationship with God.* I do not fast to *have* a relationship with God.

"Sadly, I am surprised at how many unseasoned, baby Christians shun the idea of fasting one meal as they embark on a forty day water fast, believing it will cause them to truly reach God."

Speaking of babies, how many babies or toddlers have you seen living a fasting lifestyle? No child would even survive a long fast. They not only need nourishment, they will make sure everyone around them knows they need it, too.

When we become new Christians, babies in the
Lord, we shouldn't embark on a long fasting
journey at the same time. Instead, we should take
time to develop and grow. I know there are many
new believers who are stunting their growth as
they believe and act on the fasting fad that is
sweeping the world. If you can relate with my
chapter on how not to fast, you've been fasting
too soon in your growing process.

Stunting your spiritual growth comes from
malnutrition. As we're born in God and grow, we
need an adequate amount of teaching,
nourishment and love in our relationship with
God. If this spiritual food is reduced, your
development can be delayed for life. If you are
new in God, I encourage you to grow in the Word
of God, in worship and in relationship.

Spiritual fasting can't be truly successful
without a relationship with God. Many Christians
fast to have a better relationship with God, but I
challenge you to develop that relationship first,
and then fast out of a heart that aches for Him,
His ways and His heart. Denying myself food
didn't cause me to fall in love with my husband;

our love was developed with time and communication that brought us together and enabled us to have a relationship. I know there were many meals that I missed as I wanted to talk to him for hours on end and get to know him better. But our relationship didn't flourish because I decided to do a water fast.

Could you imagine a very hungry, angry woman telling a man that he must be her boyfriend because she's been fasting for them to be a couple? Or a famished, moody man who tells a woman that they should marry because he now only eats fruits and vegetables for her? *Fasting is not the opportunity to manipulate anyone, especially God.* It's the opportunity to join in intimate relationship with another and ache for the things their heart aches for.

Relationship is key when fasting. It is essential. Let me explain it this way. Imagine that you are out running some important errands and about to stop for lunch when you get a frantic call that a loved one is in an ambulance on their way to the Emergency Room. Not just some acquaintance, but it's your child, your spouse or your parent. Think of how your heart nearly stops as your only thought is to get to them. Imagine your feelings of compassion, love and dread as you drive. Errands have become irrelevant as you rush without caution to their location. Time has stopped for you. Now imagine those feelings and think about stopping at a drive-thru to grab a sandwich. Heck, they aren't even at the ER yet; surely you could sneak a quick bite before heading there. Can you even comprehend stopping for food while your family is in danger?

"Fasting is not the opportunity to manipulate anyone, especially God. It's the opportunity to join in intimate relationship with another and ache for the things their heart aches for."

Maybe instead of the hospital, you get the call there are armed intruders at your child's school. Dangerous men have broken into the school and your child is being held hostage. Imagine the feelings, the emotions and the prayers that might come from your mouth. Feel the overwhelming intensity of the moment. Do you think you could stop for french fries? Would it even be a consideration? No! That is when true fasting and prayer kick in.

Now, imagine you're going about your busy day and flip on the news. Stories of destruction and death fill the headlines. There might even be a story about a school shooting. But you don't stop everything to pray and fight for their lives. You don't race to get to their location and think nothing of your own safety. Why? Relationship. We hear heart-wrenching stories every day, but we don't jump into action until it hits too close to home. We feel empathy and sadness, but there's a distinct difference when the story is about your own family as opposed to a complete stranger.

When Esther fasted and prayed because of the impending destruction of her people, what thoughts went through her mind when she first heard the news? Do you think of Esther as a real person with fears and emotions? Most times, as we read about the people in the Bible we think they are super-human. They never made mistakes or got afraid. But the truth is, this young girl practically had no family and even though she was in the palace, she must have felt very powerless and alone. Even in her fear, I don't believe for a second that the fasting was hard for her to do. There might've been hesitation, but the hesitation that Esther felt was due to going before the king to implore his mercy for her people. I don't think she was selfishly hesitant because she was planning an elaborate meal with her handmaidens later that night. She knew that death awaited her people. Men, women and children were going to be slaughtered at the word of a man named Haman, who wanted to annihilate the Jews. *Survival was Esther's focus, not dinner that night.* The words of Mordecai rang in her ears in Esther 4:14:

> *"And who knows but that you have come to the Kingdom for such a time as this and for this very occasion?" (AMP)*

If you knew that everyone in your family or everyone in your race was going to be slaughtered at a designated time, would you consider having lunch? Would a cookie stand in the way of your desperation to live? Food seems trivial when put into the perspective of life and death. If you were in Esther's shoes, I know that food would not have such a hold on you. You might begin calling those friends who knew how

---

"If you knew that everyone in your family or everyone in your race was going to be slaughtered at a designated time, would you consider having lunch?"

---

to pray and seek the heart of God. My bet is that your prayer life would increase exponentially; Esther's did. In Esther 4:16, she says:

"Go, gather together all the Jews that are present in Shushan, and fast for me; and neither eat nor drink for three days, night or day. I also and my maids will fast as you do. Then I will go to the king, though it is against the law: and if I perish, I perish." (AMP)

One of the most dangerous accounts of fasting and prayer was about to begin.

FASTING AND FEASTING

During Esther's fast of three days without food or water, she pushed her mind, body and spirit past countless limits. Many tears and prayers weakened her, as she turned away from food and towards her God. But Esther did more than just fast and pray. With fear and trembling, she took action.

Imagine Esther, with great physical weakness, walking past the king's military men and through the great hallways and majestic rooms of the palace, its overwhelming beauty surrounding her every step. Stunning cedar, gold and ivory designs towered above her everywhere she looked. The staggering beauty of the palace would've taken anyone's breath away, but with each step, Esther knew those could be her last moments. She was either walking to her death or

new life for her people. Psalm 23:4 describes her
moments perfectly:

*"Yes, though I walk through the [deep, sunless] valley
of the shadow of death, I will fear or dread no evil, for
You are with me; Your rod [to protect] and Your staff
[to guide], they comfort me." (AMP)*

How her heart must have been beating as
she knew the king could kill her for even entering
his presence without an invitation! Voices of the
enemy would've been forcefully trying to torment
her every step of the way. I'm sure she didn't feel
like a queen, but instead weak and alone.

Our enemy wants to destroy the people of
God. I would even dare to think that satan
himself was trying to torment and stop Esther
from bringing salvation to the Jewish people. His
words would be ringing in her ears... *'Who are
you? You're just an orphan! No one will listen. You
will be banished just like Vashti!'* He would've
known and helped implement the attack on her
people. Imagine his rage that a young, orphan
girl could thwart his plan and turn the
destruction back on him.

Esther's name literally means 'hidden.' It would have been so much easier to hide and expect someone else to rise up and bring salvation. She knew her exquisite gowns and luxurious, royal robes couldn't save her. Even her beauty and meticulous training could not bring deliverance to her people. While in the palace, she had lived a hidden lifestyle. Mordecai had warned her to not tell anyone she was Jewish, but she knew her secret was going to be revealed if she spoke to the king. By fasting and prayer she prepared herself to sacrifice her life and future, if necessary. Her actions were forbidden and deadly. Esther's eyes had to be on the Lord.

INTIMACY WITH GOD

Intimate relationship allowed Esther to walk into the presence of King Xerxes. If Esther had interrupted the king without that year of preparation and the intimacy she developed with him, she could've easily been put to death. She broke the law, knowing execution could be the penalty. Instead, her personal relationship

* * *

secured the foundation that empowered her to go places she shouldn't be permitted to go.

This is the same with God. It's an intimate relationship that will empower you to stand before our heavenly King, going places with your prayers that you shouldn't be permitted. The beautiful picture of this shows Esther standing in the presence of not one, but two kings that day. One powerful, earthly king, who reigned over the entire Persian Empire, stood before her. But our mighty, heavenly King of Kings, who rules all of existence, stood beside her. Both of them extended life to her, welcoming her into their presence. Now she had to speak for herself and the people. *Generations to come were dependent on her next words.*

PREPARING THE TABLE

Tremendous relief would have flooded Esther's heart as King Xerxes welcomed her warmly into his presence. As Esther approached and touched the end of his scepter, he spoke with great favor and love towards her:

* * *

*" 'What do you want, Queen Esther? What is your
request? I will give it to you, even if it is half the
kingdom!' And Esther replied, 'If it please the king, let
the king and Haman come today to a banquet I have
prepared for the king.'*

*The king turned to his attendants and said, 'Tell
Haman to come quickly to a banquet, as Esther has
requested.' So the king and Haman went to Esther's
banquet."* (Esther 5:3-6, NLT)

At the table, Esther sat with King Xerxes
and Haman, the king's highest official and yet the
highest enemy to Esther. How did it feel for her to
sit down with them as she knew Haman despised
Mordecai and planned death for all her people?
She also knew that by pleading with the king to
save the Jews, she would eventually reveal the
secret she had kept for so long, that she was a Jew
herself. The scriptures show us that she was a
picture of grace and hope in God, even though
she knew at the end of the banquets, one of the
attendees would be facing death, either Haman or
herself. This moment causes Psalm 23:5 to jump
off the page:

"You prepare a table before me in the presence of my enemies. You anoint my head with oil; my [brimming] cup runs over." (AMP)

Esther had the feasts ready, but God was in control of this table. He orchestrated how each banquet would go to bring salvation to his daughter, Esther. Her cup would run over with blessing. In the midst of the Jews' great distress, God prepared joyous feasts and great provision for His people. The banquet was much more than exquisite food. The meals she missed while fasting, then the meals she shared with the king and her enemy, changed the future forever. *Fasting and feasting are both vital to Esther's account.*

"The meals she missed while fasting, then the meals she shared with the king and her enemy, changed the future forever."

At the final banquet, the king asked her what she wanted once again:

* * *

"Queen Esther replied, 'If I have found favor with the King, and if it pleases the King to grant my request, I ask that my life and the lives of my people will be spared. For my people and I have been sold to those who would kill, slaughter, and annihilate us. If we had merely been sold as slaves, I could remain quiet, for that would be too trivial a matter to warrant disturbing the King.'

'Who would do such a thing?' King Xerxes demanded. 'Who would be so presumptuous as to touch you?' Esther replied, 'This wicked Haman is our adversary and our enemy.' Haman grew pale with fright before the King and Queen..." (Esther 7:3-6, NLT)

As Haman realized that Esther was a Jew, he knew his fate was sealed. In desperation, Haman begged Esther for her help, but the king commanded that Haman be put to death by the gallows he had prepared for Mordecai. And an order of the king was sent out by Mordecai that authorized all Jews to arm and defend themselves, now that he was second in command to the king.

"The King's decree gave the Jews in every city authority to unite to defend their lives. They were allowed to kill, slaughter, and annihilate anyone of any nationality or province who might attack them or their children and wives, and to take the property of their enemies." (Esther 8:11, NLT)

Haman's planned death sentence for the Jews fell back on him as Esther approached God with prayer and fasting. *Biblical fasting transforms nations, rewrites history and brings back God's order of life.* When Esther fasted and prayed, it set a celebration in motion that would last for all time. Esther 9:20-22 says:

"Mordecai recorded these events, and he sent letters to all the Jews throughout the provinces of King Xerxes, near and far, to have them celebrate annually the fourteenth and fifteenth days of the month of Adar as the time when the Jews got relief from their enemies, and as the month when their sorrow was turned into joy and their mourning into a day of celebration." (NIV)

The book of Esther introduces us to a lowly, orphan girl hidden in the palace. All of us are like

Esther and have a *'hidden salvation'* ready to emerge. Esther didn't start out as a queen. She was an orphan without anything to offer anyone. She was taken into the palace much like we are taken into the Kingdom of God as we become new Christians. As she steps out by fasting and prayer, she causes a ricochet that the world will forever rejoice in, knowing the rescuing power of our God! She is no longer hidden, but celebrating publicly how God delivered her people! The book of Esther is a picture of true biblical fasting.

WHERE IS YOUR ACHE?

If I were to poll every person on the face of the earth asking what fasting means, a large percentage would define it with one word - *denial.* Some believe that it is the denial of food, while others explain it as a spiritual discipline or abstaining from doing something enjoyable. Almost every religion has a set of days to fast and give up something you desire for a period of time. While I do commend those who are doing the best with what they know, my desire is to give a greater understanding of the power of true, biblical fasting.

How would Esther define it? I can imagine her speaking to her children and grandchildren about the fateful day she courageously walked into the presence of the king after three days of fasting and prayer. Did she recount all the ways her body ached or how she was craving sweets? Was food her focus? I don't think so. Her words wouldn't recall the meals she missed, but instead the closeness of her God and His rescuing power.

And what would Esther think of our fasting today? I believe she would be shocked at how powerless we've made it. Essentially, we've turned fasting into something that is virtually ineffective in a world that's crying out for the real, tangible presence of God to come down and rescue. I believe her heart would break, wishing that we would understand the truth of how powerful fasting and prayer can be. And I join her, knowing we are only scratching the surface of all God wants to do.

Like her, we need God's beauty treatments. Our hearts need softening and the deception of the world must be cleansed away by the Lord. And after a season, with maturity, we begin to hear the cries of the people. They are crying out for someone to fast and pray. Esther's actions saved an entire nation that faced certain destruction. Remember, Esther's name is still being spoken today because of the sacrifice she made; without that, we wouldn't even know her name. Someone else would have arisen and brought salvation for God's people.

Is your book being written? Is someone else stepping into the destiny God planned for you because you don't respond with fasting and prayer? Do *not* let your story be given to another —someone more willing than you!

Destruction is pressing down upon us all. Your enemy is looking to annihilate anyone he can get his hands on. Do we need to be praying and fasting for the human race? Yes! Does your church, country, city or family need God to intervene and rescue? Absolutely!

Now, don't get me wrong, we all know fasting can put your body through a lot of unpleasantries, but if your focus and ache are for the Lord, you won't notice all the discomforts. When I first started fasting, I could easily recognize when my body reacted negatively. Why? Because that was my main focus. One way to test your spiritual fasting is to ask yourself, *'After the fast, do I remember all the things God has done, or do I remember how I craved food more than I craved the Word of God?'* Many of my own memories are filled with the time I spent with my thoughts and negotiations of food rather than the Word during the fast.

I began to seek the Lord, asking what I was doing wrong. And He gave me one word, *ache.* The word *'ache'* is very diverse. Everyone has felt this emotion as they've fasted, whether it be a stomach ache, body ache or heartache. I put together three types of ache that people experience while fasting, as all ache isn't created equal. And it doesn't produce the same response or outcome. Let me break down the first two types, in the following acronyms:

Legalistic Ache	Immature Ache
Argumentative	Aimless
Ceremonial	Counterfeit
Hypocritical	Heartbreaking
Elite	Exhausting

As I fasted, I bounced back and forth from a Legalistic Ache to an Immature Ache for many years. Even though I was so sincere in my actions, the enemy showed me a form of fasting that divided me from God and was powerless in its working. It was counterfeit and easily overtaken by my flesh. I can see myself in each of the descriptive words in the above table.

I didn't step into a Godly Ache until I developed an intimate relationship with God and had the understanding that fasting was an ache — an ache that was active in prayer, courageously close to God, humble and empowered. As these words started to become alive in me, I began experiencing biblical results!

Godly Ache
Active in Prayer
Courageously Close
Humble
Empowered

People in the Bible fasted knowing that real enemies were after them, or that they needed to turn to God in repentance, or that there was a desperate need for God to intervene. Biblical fasting was not casual. It took great courage for Esther to turn to the Lord and lay her life before

Him, knowing He was the only one who could save her.

"Is someone else stepping into the destiny God planned for you because you don't respond with fasting and prayer?"

When I finally realized I first needed to have a tangible, developed relationship with God and then add the powerful, God-given gift of fasting, God was able to move much more powerfully on my behalf than I had ever imagined. It was like throwing gasoline on a fire! The spark was always there, but it needed to be empowered. Fasting, praying and believing that God was going to move in my life and the lives of others, caused an explosive reaction.

A CITY'S DESPERATE CRY

In every nation there are people who go without food as they have no other choice. Homeless people are starving in the streets of our own country. Are they fasting? Does *not* eating make you spiritual? There are others who are driven not to eat because all they can see is how fat they think they are. Does their choice to go without food make them godly? Absolutely not. Yet, many Christians believe, *'As long as I'm not eating, God hears me.'*

Fasting and prayer must be an ache that includes turning to our God, not just turning away from food. When we turn to something, we receive it in its entirety. We capture and lay hold of it. 2 Chronicles 7:14 says:
"If my people, who are called by my name, will humble themselves and pray and seek my face and turn from their wicked ways, then I will hear from heaven, and I will forgive their sin and will heal their land." (NLT)

One of the keys to this scripture is *if.* If we humble ourselves and pray, seek and turn, then He will hear, forgive and heal. This is a picture of what the king and the people of Nineveh did. Prayer should be so full of faith and expectation that it is like turning on a faucet and expecting water to come out.

* * *

"Prayer should be so full of faith and expectation that it is like turning on a faucet and expecting water to come out."

God told His prophet, Jonah, to warn Nineveh that destruction was coming to their city if they didn't repent. Nineveh was a very prosperous place and considered one of the more sophisticated cities of its time, three days' journey in width. It was also known to be a very violent region where bloodshed, mayhem and idolatry were plentiful. Today, monuments still exist in museums that boast of the great cruelty of the people, which include burning enemies alive and cutting off people's heads, forming them into pillars. But as Jonah spoke the Word of the Lord, there was an astonishing and heartfelt reaction from the king. Jonah 3:6-10 says:

"When the King of Nineveh heard what Jonah was saying, he stepped down from his throne and took off his royal robes. He dressed himself in burlap and sat on a heap of ashes. Then the King and his nobles sent

50

this decree throughout the city:

'No one, not even the animals from your herds and flocks, may eat or drink anything at all. People and animals alike must wear garments of mourning, and everyone must pray earnestly to God. They must turn from their evil ways and stop all their violence. Who can tell? Perhaps even yet God will change His mind and hold back His fierce anger from destroying us.' When God saw what they had done and how they had put a stop to their evil ways, He changed His mind and did not carry out the destruction He had threatened." (NLT)

More than 120,000 people were saved when they turned to God with prayer and fasting. They believed Jonah immediately and repented. How many times do we forget the response of the people of Nineveh as we focus on Jonah? This is a tremendous testimony of an entire city, one of the largest of its era, feeling the ache of God and turning to Him as one. In life and death situations like this, fasting is a powerful force as you respond to God's warnings. The Lord made the first move towards the Ninevites as he sent Jonah to warn them of destruction. Even in the midst of

minimal relationship, the people turned their
hearts to God with passionate repentance and
God was moved by their heartfelt sincerity.

Comparing it to our time, it would be like
Baghdad, Iraq, hearing the Word of the Lord from
a prophet and everyone immediately humbling
themselves, seeking His face and turning from
their wicked ways.

How would the King of Nineveh describe
fasting and prayer? What a shock it must've been
to the people to watch him come down from his
throne, take off his stunning, royal robes and turn
to God. In that moment, he was transformed! He
would tell you that earnest, heartfelt prayer and
fasting can change God's mind. It can even
deflect the wrath of God. Have you fasted like
that yet? I want you to know, you can.

MOSES' DESIRE FOR THE GLORY

What would Moses say about the first forty
days he spent fasting on Mount Sinai with God?
Would he share what his body experienced as he
went without food and water? Would he feel

pretty proud of himself that he fasted longer than anyone else he knew?

"If Moses studied most of the teaching that is available on fasting today, it wouldn't have prepared him for the magnificent, life-altering moments with God."

Or instead, would he describe the overwhelming moments of the Lord speaking with him? Or how he knew God wrote the Ten Commandments on the tablets with His own finger? Maybe he would tell how the glory of the Lord overpowered every fiber of his being as the mountain shook and roared like a raging fire without burning him. Now *that* is someone I would love to have teach me about fasting and prayer!

As Moses spent time with God on the mountain, he was learning the secrets and blueprints of the Kingdom. God was sharing the layout and needs of the Tent of Meeting, the place where He would dwell and live among His people. The Lord describes it in Exodus 29:43-46:

*"There I will meet with the Israelites and the Tent of Meeting shall be sanctified by My glory, the Shekinah, God's visible presence… I will **dwell** among the Israelites and be their God. And they shall **know** [from personal experience] that I am the Lord their God, who brought them forth out of the land of Egypt that I might dwell among them; I am the Lord their God." (AMP)*

If Moses studied most of the teaching that is available on fasting today, it wouldn't have prepared him for the magnificent, life-altering moments with God. He might've told God he needed a few days to purge his tent of all desserts and have a final smorgasbord of his favorite foods before heading up the mountain. But instead, the moment Moses started walking up the side of Mount Sinai, he was stepping out of any legalistic or immature *ache* and into the very presence of God.

I WILL PERISH ALSO

As the Israelites waited on the return of Moses, they became impatient and went to Aaron telling him they wanted him to make a god for themselves. Giving in, not only did Aaron take all their gold jewelry to shape an idol, but he also built an altar for it and proclaimed a feast for the following day. As the calf was revealed in Exodus 32, Aaron said, " *'These are your gods, O Israel, which brought you up out of the land of Egypt!'* "(AMP)

Near the same time, God told Moses:

" *'Quick! Go down the mountain! Your people whom you brought from the land of Egypt have corrupted themselves... Now leave me alone so my fierce anger can blaze against them, and I will destroy them. Then I will make you, Moses, into a great nation.'* "
(Exodus 32:7, 9, NLT)

As Moses was spending precious time in the presence of God, experiencing great revelation, he was participating in a supernatural sustenance we *can't even comprehend.* This meant

Moses was supplied with all the necessities and nourishment his body, mind and spirit needed... by God! Then picture the Lord telling him to go back down Mount Sinai because the people had corrupted themselves, worshiping a golden calf. Moses easily could've stayed more than forty days on the mountain, in the overwhelming glory of God, had Aaron and the people not built that golden calf! The people chose a lifeless statue of a *farm animal* over the God Who had protected them, saved them and delivered them from over four hundred years of oppressive enslavement!

"As he fasted, Moses was supplied with all the necessities and nourishment his body, mind and spirit needed... by God!"

We cannot even begin to understand how this angered God! God was so upset with the people that He didn't tell Moses to go down to 'MY' people, but to go down to 'YOUR' people. God was saying to Moses, *'Those people are no longer Mine, they are not of Me. I loved them with a passionate, sacrificial love; I gave them everything!*

And they betrayed Me. Now I am no longer their God!'

As Moses came down the mountain and confronted Aaron about the sin of the people, Aaron said in Exodus 32:22-24:

" 'Don't get so upset, my lord…You yourself know how evil these people are. They said to me, "Make us gods who will lead us. We don't know what happened to this fellow Moses, who brought us here from the land of Egypt." So I told them, "Whoever has gold jewelry, take it off." When they brought it to me, I simply threw it into the fire – and out came this calf!' " (NLT)

Pardon? You just threw in the gold and out came a golden calf? And these people made you throw gold into the fire to give them a god? Aaron's words immediately place blame on Moses and the people as he says, *'You yourself know how evil these people are.'* It is apparent that Aaron does not have a passion or ache for God's people. He is quick to place blame anywhere other than himself. He is trying to save himself. At this point he would have told God to wipe them out and start over again. Whereas, in verse 30-32, Moses returned to the Lord and said:

" 'Oh, what a terrible sin these people have committed. They have made gods of gold for themselves. But now, if You will only forgive their sin – but if not, erase my name from the record You have written!' " (NLT)

Moses' heart for the people is evident in these words. 'If You would only forgive their sin – but if not, erase my name from the record You have written!' The record Moses was referring to was the Book of Life. Moses was not even near the sin that was committed, yet he was willing to lose his life for many others. That is a picture of a Godly Ache!

Even though the golden calf was being built by everyone else, Moses was willing to stand in the gap, volunteering to be blotted out of God's book. He wasn't there, yet he came down and said, 'Maybe I can go up and make atonement for you. Blot me out. Take my life if you must.' This is true fasting and prayer. Again, we hear words like Esther's: 'If Israel is to perish, I will perish also.' Moses didn't make excuses, he was the atonement that was willing to stand between a sinful people and a God who was ready to destroy them.

The Words I Didn't Want to Hear

      I have been a faithful church attender since birth. I sang the songs, bowed my head at the appropriate times and considered myself a good Christian girl. But for the first half of my life, I didn't have a true relationship with God. I didn't know Him. I grew up in churches where there was an implied understanding that all Christians fasted and prayed. No one would dare admit that they hadn't prayed daily. At least everyone had prayed the 'negotiation prayer' during a test or when they needed God to do something extraordinary for them.

      Yet the first life-changing, breakthrough prayer I remember hearing was my own, when I asked Jesus into my heart in Sunday School. I was eight or nine years old and the teacher told us that we could ask Jesus into our hearts. She explained that she would lead us in a prayer after class if we wanted to stay. My teacher, Fawn, was unlike anyone I'd ever met. She had a kindness and love for God that drew me in. As my heart softened towards the Lord, I stayed behind when all the kids quickly rushed back to their parents after the class.

After that moment, there was so much I wanted to learn and become! I didn't understand all I was doing as I asked Jesus into my heart, but I knew a real desire to know God had awakened in me. Even as I said my first prayer, I'd hoped that after that day I wouldn't struggle to love God. But not much changed as I made every effort through the years to be the 'good girl.' Sadly, I never experienced breakthrough prayers in church again until I was sixteen years old, and I remember that night very vividly.

"COME TO HER FOR PRAYER!"

It was *'Revival Week'* at our church and an evangelist from out of town was preaching, sweating, and stirring the crowd. It was such a sight to our congregation who had faithfully strived to keep every service at a high standard of holiness and calm reverence. In our services, I only remember the prayers of an elderly, missionary-type lady who would say the name of Jesus over and over and over... and over again.

As the evangelist concluded his sermon later that night, he began to walk among the people heading directly toward my mother and me. With each step he took, I felt as though I was watching someone move in slow motion. I could hear him speaking, but had no idea what he was saying. I was horrified, yet mesmerized, that he had singled me out of the entire congregation.

Soon he was towering before us and I thought I was literally going to pass out. At sixteen, I wasn't a rebellious teenager but I knew that this man of God was standing before my mother to tell her all that I had done wrong. Every sin, every bad thought and every lie was about to be exposed to all who could hear. For the first time in my life, I truly was experiencing the fear of the Lord.

Then he began to speak, and it was actually much worse than I had thought. With my mother's permission to speak over me he said, *'First of all, this young girl is a prayer warrior. And not only is she a prayer warrior for God, but she is going to go places that no one else will go. She is going to give in ways that no one else will give, and she is going to pray and fast in ways that others will not.'*

Immediately, my mind began to swirl with pictures of third-world countries, humid jungles and back alleys. Where was I going to pray? Where were those places that no one else would go? *This could not be good!* There was probably a very good reason that people didn't go to those places! I was overwhelmed with dread of what God had in store for me.

The evangelist continued on with great vigor, *'God wants to get her equipped. She needs to practice. She is not prepared for what is coming and she must pray for people!'* He then gazed out over the congregation and nearly ordered them to come to me for prayer so I could begin the preparation. He then looked at the pastor and said, *'Make sure she experiences prayer! She needs to practice now!'*

Could it have gotten any worse? I began to wish that instead he had let the entire world know all my secret sins. What about the times I had lied to my mom? Why not speak of all my faults? He kept repeating with a booming voice, *'She needs to practice. She needs an opportunity to pray. Come to her for prayer! Help her become prepared. She is a prayer warrior for God!'*

Believe me, it didn't get easier with repetition. I had never really prayed in my life. He might as well have said that I was going to build the Golden Gate Bridge by myself... overnight! I wondered if he had checked with God about this so-called *'word'* for me.

Did people begin to jump at the chance to have a sixteen-year-old farm girl pray for them? No. Did anyone take me under their wing and teach me how to pray? No. Did I then begin that work of becoming equipped to pray? No. Even with the evangelist's repetitive, spit-filled pleading and encouragements to the pastor and the people to allow me the chance to practice prayer—not one person ever approached me, nor did anyone from the church ever bring up the subject after that night, including myself.

To the congregation, it was as if it never happened, but inside of me, something new had been awakened. Could there really be a people who were able to pray and connect with God? Could I learn to pray for people and see them get better? Would I ever find a catalyst to help me become who I was supposed to be?

A TRUE CATALYST

It wasn't until the day I walked into Smithton Community Church, when I was twenty years old, that I was able to connect with God. Previously, there had been no catalyst. All my attempts at prayer and fasting were held back. I had never known exactly what I had been searching for but suddenly I knew I had found it.

So what exactly is a catalyst? According to the dictionary, the definition for *'catalyst'* is:

* * *

1. Material that empowers a chemical reaction to advance at an unusually faster rate or under different conditions than otherwise were achievable

2. An substance that enables or speeds significant change or action

When I was able to get in contact with a church that believed and prayed in the power and authority of God, I found my catalyst! I began to grow at a faster rate and watched my prayers experience significant change and action.

However, it didn't happen overnight. I can remember praying with such heart and sincerity, and sputtering out within seconds of starting. My prayers sounded like I was a baby in the Lord... and I was! How could I talk for hours on end with my friends and have nothing to say to God? My fasting attempts weren't much better. I remember deciding to fast and eating something within hours, and sometimes minutes.

Many days I would walk our land or sit in my family's barn, asking God to help me pray.

Prayer can be hard to develop. It takes desire and work, but as you pray over and over again, you will begin to crave it. You will want your life to be free and clear of the debris that so easily works itself in without daily prayer and relationship with God. Prayer began to restore my awareness of how much I desperately needed God. It also made me much more wise to the darkness that tried to stick around and wedge itself deep into my life.

HUNGRY TO PRAY

Since the day I found my catalyst, I have been learning how to fast and pray. It seems so effortless and simple to say that I have been learning to pray; but that statement is so powerful, weighty and precious. It has forever changed my life and countless lives around me. It's the kind of prayer and fasting that pulls down the presence of God and brings life where there was death. It's the kind of prayer that turns the hearts of people back to their God. Truly, it's the kind of prayer that changes how history would have been written. It's prayer with results.

It's not prayer that says, *'I'll remember you in my prayers,'* and then goes home and never prays for the need at all. And it's not prayer that says, *'Lord, let your will be done and heal as you see fit.'*

It's a kind of prayer that stops and says, *'We must pray right now!'* It's a purposeful prayer that's bold and stands in for another. It's prayer that strikes with such a force that it opens what was closed before. It doesn't take *'no'* for an answer and it continues to strike until walls of fear, disease and hopelessness are broken down.

You might be thinking, *'Wow... this sounds so forceful, so intense; I might not be ready to pray like that.'* There is coming a day that you might need to pray with raw intensity to see God come down and help someone close to you. Do not wait for that day! Be in training now. Begin the journey.

If you visit any hospital, you'll see desperate people in prayer. They might be untrained and unfamiliar with prayer entirely. It could be that they have never prayed in their lives. Go to any emergency room and you will

* * *

hear the sounds of urgent cries that will reach the heart of God. But do not wait for that day!

Let me take a moment to repeat these catalyst words over YOU. These words are not for a person, but for a people:

You are called to be a prayer warrior. You are called to go places that no one else will go, called to give in ways that no one else will give and called to pray in ways that no one else will pray.

God wants you equipped. You need to practice. You might not be prepared for what's coming, and you must begin to pray and fast for people.

Are you ready to begin a journey of true prayer and fasting that sees results?

Breaking the Grip of Heartache

The next few chapters were hard for me to write. I avoided writing about my father as long as I could. Many times I have shared this story in lectures or with friends, but it was much more *painfully real* to write it out on paper. This experience shaped my life and who I have become, and I am thankful for it.

Some of my greatest childhood memories were spent working on my parents' farm. My dad would always say, *'The family that works together, sticks together.'* During those years, I remember driving tractors before I could even see over the steering wheel and in the winter, being chased by cows as my sister and I rode on sleds pulled behind my dad's pick-up truck.

Summers were even busier as my family would walk miles and miles through fields cutting down shattercane in the hottest months and shucking more corn than I can imagine. And I spent more time with hogs than with people, saving them from the brutal heat. Bitterly cold, wet weather during the calving season always meant newborn calves would be brought on our back porch. As we used our own personal towels to dry them off, we were saving their lives. My father believed in hard work for all of us and there were no brothers to share the load.

My father was the strongest man I had ever known; a man who owned and successfully operated a debt-free, 1,200-acre farm. We had over five hundred head of cattle and sixty sows that produced two hundred baby pigs twice a year. We had crops to tend, fences to fix and always a herd of cats. In my nineteen years of life, I had never seen him sick. Not once. Ever. This was a man who worked every single day. Farmers don't get personal days or sick days. At least my father didn't; not until the doctors diagnosed him with cancer at age forty-seven.

At that point in my life, I was just beginning to realize how much my parents had always sacrificed for me, and I was becoming wise enough to ask advice. I was growing up— becoming a woman, and not just a child. My home life wasn't always the easiest, but I knew I needed my father.

My life as a farm girl gave me some of my happiest memories, but that life was about to drastically change. The first report from the doctors showed that my father had two inoperable tumors: one on his spine, pressing on his sciatic nerve and the other on his bladder. He went through a week of radiation and then at the second MRI, they tested his face. It showed that cancer was throughout his sinuses. They didn't test any further. As my father told my mother the cancer was in his face, it was the only time she saw him cry about the diagnosis. The results were evident that the cancer was throughout his body. I watched his strong, hard-working figure start to disappear rapidly as the days went by.

Initially I remember being in shock, thinking that the fight was over. There was nothing to be done. Radiation and chemotherapy were not going to work. That was it. He was going to die. Then a few days later, a group of people from our church came by the house to pray for my father. Many of them didn't know him, because he had not attended a service at our church. My father had sworn to my mother that he would never enter the doors of our church. Most of my teenage life, I remember my mother fighting for us to be able to go to church and then fighting with him again when we got home.

The night the church members came to our house, I vividly remember being afraid that they had even shown up. My dad wasn't ever keen on unexpected guests. And when they had the courage to ask my father if he would like to be give his life to God, I thought I would fall through the floor! But in one swift moment, he said yes! I thought I must have been dreaming!

I felt like saying, *'I'm sorry Dad... did you understand the question?'* I had given up hope and hardened my heart many years earlier. In my own pain from all the fighting, I had shut down a part of myself that would believe that my father would ever open his heart to God. My mother had prayed and believed for this moment for years, but I was in shock that it was even happening. The day was finally here that he would experience God for himself.

Some of you know of a loved one that you have cried and prayed over for years. Don't give up! *May God intervene and bring salvation to your family and friends!*

I couldn't believe it, but he had said yes! I looked around the room and realized that not one of the church members was moving toward him to pray. He had been lying on the couch the entire time, unable to get up from the pain. I think they were as stunned as I was! They asked if they could pray, but they weren't sure what to do after that!

With tears in my eyes, I went to our couch and knelt beside him, putting my hand on his arm. In that instant, my father quickly clasped my hand, squeezed it, and more tears ran down my face. It was a true act of affection, something I hadn't done in a very long time. The hesitant church group then came and put their hands on me. I felt walls of protection falling away, my heart softening and breaking as the grip of heartache left my body. Quickly, joy flooded my soul. I was brand new. *In that moment, my life was saved as much as his.* His first words after the prayer were, *'I feel so clean.'* I watched my father transform instantly before my very eyes—all of the hurt, disappointment and anger I felt toward him melted away. He had become a new man.

A new man... dying of cancer. How could this be?

As the church group was leaving the house, my sister, Christina, came in the house and saw a Bible on our dad's chest. Knowing that even slight pressure was painful to his body, she immediately went over to remove it. His eyes popped open and he grasped the Bible tighter, stopping her, *'No, honey, leave it there. I have a glow.'* She said, *'But, Dad, it's too heavy.'* He answered, *'No, it's not. It's light now!'* This same man, just a hour before, wouldn't have had a

Bible near him. My father's salvation was nothing short of miraculous. But our journey was just the beginning of all God had in store for us.

FAITH CAME ALIVE

Even as the doctors gave my father no hope to survive, suddenly faith for healing came alive inside my mother and me. We knew that God would heal him. It was not even a question of *if* He could. We knew that HE WOULD!

Over the course of the next few weeks, despite the disease, my father experienced God in ways that I had never seen anyone ever experience the Lord.

The very day he said a prayer asking God to save him, my mother immediately went to find the Bible she had bought him many years ago. As she eagerly handed it to him, shame filled his face. The beauty of the leather, the clean, gold-trimmed pages, and the lack of use were too much for him. *'Please go and grab your worn and weathered Bible,'* he said to my mom. *'That's the type of Bible I want to use.'*

Soon after that, he told my mother that he wanted to be baptized in water. Even though he was in excruciating pain, the men of our church carried his shrunken body to our bathtub. At this point my father couldn't walk anymore. As they laid him back on the hospital bed in my parents' room, bruises were instantly forming on his body from moving him. Concerned, the men of the church asked him if he was alright. My father looked at them with tears in his eyes and said, *'I've never felt better in my whole life.'*

On the following Wednesday evening, I walked into my mom and dad's bedroom. Only my father and I were there. As I walked through the door, I felt like I was bumping into people and even stepping on their toes. Approaching my dad, I said without thinking, *'There are so many angels in here I could hardly get to you!'* He didn't seem the least bit surprised. Just then the phone rang. I answered it, and it was our pastor's wife. She said, *'I never do this, but I had to briefly leave Wednesday evening service to call and tell you, there are so many angels at your house that they can't be*

* * *

numbered!' Tears sprang to my eyes as I knew God was showing His goodness to me.

My father also had wonderful dreams of walking and talking with Jesus. As he would awaken, he would tell my mother of things that Jesus had said, mysteries of God that we had never heard, but would later find in the Word of God.

My father was well-known throughout the area as a prosperous businessman. As word spread that he was sick, powerful men from all over came to visit. After their time with him, they would leave the room with shocked looks on their faces. One man even brought a Bible the second time he visited my father. Even though he was unable to move from the bed, his words were strong and impacting.

Throughout all the excruciating pain that my father was feeling, he never stopped loving God with all his heart. On Father's Day, he told us that he was going to church to honor his heavenly Father. He had sworn that he would never step foot in church, yet he was there showing God his love and devotion. I can still see him sitting in the pew beside us, unable to stand in worship because of the pain. But he was there!

The following day, my mother took my father to see the pain specialist. The doctors had planned for a morphine drip to be inserted directly into his back to ease the pain. As the specialist asked my father how his pain level was on a scale of one to ten the day before, my father said it was an eleven. My father went to church in intolerable pain. At one point during the service, he even had to take liquid morphine. Most people won't go to church if they have the sniffles or even if they're tired. On Sunday mornings many well-intentioned Christians are still in bed, but serving God isn't about intentions. As I watched my father, I realized this was a man who loved God more than he loved himself.

Without realizing it, my father was one of the biggest catalysts in my life. I have never met anyone like him who loved God so deeply and sincerely. Seeing my dad like this stretched me. It changed me. And so did his death.

Death Has No Hold

On July 15th, 1998, my father had to have
emergency surgery. The nurse who had been
taking care of him at my parents' home had
incorrectly inserted his catheter. As a result of
that, my father's bladder swelled to such a great
size that the doctors thought it had burst. They
even said they were concerned all the organs in
his body were bursting. Thankfully they hadn't;
but after the surgery, bruising completely covered
him from the waist down.

The doctors told my mother that he was
going to die within five days and wanted to keep
him in the hospital. But my mother said, *'No, he's
going home.'* Without hesitation, neither my
mother nor I was wavering in faith that my father
was going to be healed. At that point, our faith

* * *

was so steadfast, we believed if he died, he would be brought back to life.

It was as if you could tell me that the sky was blue, the leaves were green, and my father was going to be healed. I believed, without any uncertainty, that he was going to be made whole. God had somehow planted an unshakable belief in me, and it *did not* waver.

The day he died, July 22nd, I was in Sedalia, Missouri, where I had been attending college. My sister was walking through the room where my father was lying on a hospital bed, when he called out to her. For the few days prior, since the operation, he had not eaten, had not drunk any liquids or been able to speak. But, as she was walking through the room, he called out, *'Pray for me.'* And then she watched as he took his last breath.

He was gone.

But that didn't stop the faith we had in God. As my sister, Christina, called me on the phone to tell me that Dad had died, I felt a surge of anticipation that my father was going to be healed that day! Death did not alter God's plan for life. Our faith outweighed death!

As I drove from Sedalia to Amoret, I didn't mourn or cry. The two hours flew by as I thought of how great it was going to be to be able to hug and touch my father again. For those weeks that he was sick, he was unable to be touched without experiencing excruciating pain. My heart was soaring as I knew that there was going to be a great celebration of his healing.

When I reached my parents' property, my body became so heavy that I couldn't walk. I had never experienced anything like that in my life. As my sister and mother helped me to the house, I felt an overwhelming presence of God that literally made my body feel weighed down. I couldn't comprehend what was happening, but knew I was going to see my father soon!

A few friends and family members joined my mother, sister and me in prayer. We continued to believe and expect God to heal his body and raise it from the dead. For the next few hours, we praised God and expected the miracle. At different times, I walked into my parents' bedroom and spent time praying over my father.

A few days before his death, a tumor on the right side of his forehead had grown so large that it pushed down against his eyebrow; even changing the way his face looked. It was painfully shocking to actually *see* the cancer. Here was this evil disease showing itself. Every time I saw it, great anger rose up inside of me. But as I looked at him on his bed, I saw that the tumor was gone.

Anyone who knows someone diagnosed with cancer, knows how enraged you can get at something you can't even see. As I wanted to destroy the cancer within my father, I pictured myself having the chance to take it into another room. It might sound crazy, but I wanted remove it and to beat cancer to a pulp; to destroy it, even if it was with my bare hands. If only there were something I could've done… I would've gladly given my life to kill it.

THE VISION

After those few hours of prayer, two men knocked on the front door. These two men, whom none of us knew, said God had told them to find the man who needed to be raised from the dead. As they drove around inquiring, they were pointed to our house. Instantly, we invited them in. It sounds like a radical idea, doesn't it? We didn't question it. We didn't wonder how these two men knew what we were praying. We knew God was answering our prayers.

As time passed, the men asked if they could go into the bedroom where my father lay. My mother agreed, and we continued praying in the living room. After a few minutes, one of them returned and said that he had seen a vision.

At that point in my life, I had never experienced greater faith for anything. My heart was set, and I knew that my father was going to be healed. Any other answer would have crushed my entire belief system. *If what you believe in, more than anything, turns out to be untrue… what's left to believe?*

The man began to share how he saw my father standing with Jesus. He said it looked like they were at the end of a long corridor looking down at us. Jesus said to my father, *'Look down there.'* After looking at us, my father turned to Jesus and asked, *'What are they doing?'* Then Jesus turned to him and said, *'They are praying for your return.'*

I know that some of you who are reading this have experienced the death of a loved one; someone who died prematurely from sickness or an accident. Many people can't understand the injustice of death, and I don't have the answers. But I do know that my father's answer to Jesus saved me.

As my father looked at us and then at Jesus, he asked four simple words: *'Do I have to?'* His words struck my heart like a sledgehammer. In that moment everyone in the room felt the release to let him go. My mother immediately said, *'No, we let him go. We release him. He is with Jesus. Who would want to leave Jesus?'*

* * *

NO TURNING BACK

The picture of where my father was seemed so clear. He was where he wanted to be. He wasn't coming back, and I wanted to let him stay. As I walked into my parents' bedroom again to say goodbye, the peace of God was so strong. I looked at my father's face and it glowed so brightly; it was truly evident that he was with Jesus!

As I cried, I pulled back the sheets and looked at my father's body. I yearned to be able to keep him near me. I didn't want to forget him. I wanted to remember his long feet, his pale farmer's legs and dark brown arms and face. I touched the large scar on his upper chest that he always told me was from a knife fight, but I knew it wasn't true. I held his hand and hugged him. While he had been sick, any physical touch was painful for him. I hadn't been able to hug him for weeks. As I put my head on his chest, I noticed that he was still warm and that his arms and legs weren't stiff.

He had passed away around ten in the morning, and when I felt his chest, it was after five that night. I touched his forehead, again noticing the absence of the tumor that had earlier distorted his face. Days later a woman from our church told us that she saw a vision of Jesus kissing my father's forehead around the same time that he had passed away. When we asked her which side it was on, she said the exact place where the tumor had been, without knowing about the tumor at all. *Jesus' kiss dissolved that tumor.*

STATE OF WAITING

Soon after that, we called to have my father's body taken to the funeral home. The coroner, who was a family friend, told my sister that he had dreaded picking him up. With the many hours my father had been in the air-conditioned room, the coroner knew it would be hard to drain his body of blood. He even told my mother that we couldn't have an open casket due to the complications he would have draining the blood. When a person passes away, their blood must be emptied to prepare the body for burial.

But miraculously, the coroner told us that when he began to drain my father's blood, it was like he had died five minutes prior and not seven hours earlier.

My father's body was put in a state of waiting. Our prayers worked. They gave my father a chance to make a choice. I know cancer left his body and God gave us the answer we were looking for.

To this day, I will never forget the faith God gave me for my father. I had a relentless faith that would not take no for an answer. Thousands of times since then, I've had the chance to pray for people. I've seen countless miracles and hundreds of people healed of cancer. There is no greater feeling than praying and watching God rescue lives. And as I do, I can still sometimes hear the Lord say, '*Heather, remember the faith you had for your father.*'

IGNITING THE PASSION

The day my father died will be forever etched in my memory. It was one of the hardest, and one of the best, days of my life. Throughout the many years, my heart has ached for a chance to see my father again. Heaven has become a much more real place — a place I intend to go not only to see my heavenly Father, but also to see my father that was here on Earth. And, even though it's been seventeen years, I still long for him in my life. I watch other fathers hug their daughters and ache for something that can no longer be. And I know I'm not the only one with that ache. Many of you have experienced such heartache, and long for a reunion of those you have lost.

Years ago in a church service, my pastor, Steve Gray, began speaking to our congregation about hurts and broken areas of life that we were carrying. *'You don't have to carry this yourself. You aren't designed to carry all that weight. You weren't created to carry the pain from the death of loved ones.'* His words were cutting through a layer that had kept me in a deep sorrow.

As he did, my heart became like wax and I began to feel the sadness again of losing my father. After the diagnosis, I had only five weeks with my father before he died. I felt anger rise up within me. I was robbed of the time I needed with him. As my heart broke, it was as if Jesus was saying it was okay that I yearned to see him again; it was okay that I missed him with every fiber of my being. Slowly, I let myself feel the pain. The rawness of it started to come through. As it did, I told God I would do anything; *anything* to spend time with my father again. If I could just have one hour with him I would scale tall buildings, fight sharks, or walk through fire to reach him. I knew it wasn't possible to see him, but that was my heart's cry.

My sobs began to overtake me as I allowed myself to feel the pain and desire. Again, I began 'negotiating' with God. If only I could have thirty minutes with him... twenty minutes... ten minutes... even one minute. How my heart would soar to spend a minute with my father, whom I had loved and lost. My body, mind, and spirit were overcome with the agonizing need to reach him. I realized that I was consumed with this yearning to be with my earthly father, and Jesus was comforting me with compassion. Jesus' heart was breaking for me, too.

Then, I began to picture what I would do if I knew my father was in the building. I could see myself scaling walls or breaking through any obstacle in my way to be near him. I wouldn't be wondering what anyone thought. I wouldn't wait to see if it was the right thing to do! My passion to reach him would override all common sense. I would even give my life to see him again. Failure to find him would not be an option; *nothing* would stand in my way.

Then, it was as if Jesus was speaking directly to me. While in the midst of the tears and vows to do whatever it took to reach my father, Jesus was saying, 'Now... *take that desire, that pain, and that willingness to do anything to reach your dad and give it to Me. Make that desire for Me.'*

What a moment! It was all so very clear. I could see anew into the spiritual realm. Now I knew how to take a feeling that was meant to destroy me, and turn it into a means to empower me. It felt like I suddenly knew how to reach the throne of God. Prayer was not just a conversation. Would I speak to my earthly father like it was an everyday occurrence? No! Now I realized I could never talk to God like that either. A new world had been opened up, and freeing revelation had come. I was alive like never before!

To be with God, I didn't need to plead and hope. I could have a relationship with Him at any time. I didn't need to negotiate for an hour or even one minute. He was mine, right now. Words like *yearn*, *thirst*, *long*, and *crave* began to make such perfect sense. Words like these:

"My soul THIRSTS for God, for the living God. When can I go and meet with God?" (Psalm 42:2, NIV)

"My soul YEARNS for you in the night; my spirit within me earnestly SEEKS you." (Isaiah 26:9, NLT)

These are words from someone who has a passion for God. These are words of someone who is searching for God with fervency. Look for Him. He can be found! He longs to be with you!

This is how our heavenly Father desires to be with us as well! He isn't saying that we need to scale tall buildings and put our lives at risk to be with Him. He just wants to know that we would be willing to do anything to reach Him. As we draw near to Him, He draws near to us. This isn't just a casual movement by God; He rushes toward us with urgency and love!

I challenge you to be vulnerable before the Lord. Open your heart to Him and He will open His heart to you! Let nothing stand in your way as you reach out to Him and your life will be forever changed!

GIVE YOURSELF TO HEALING

For the past twelve years, I have been part of a prayer ministry called 'The House of Hope and Healing.' It's a place for people to call or visit to receive prayer, and it's open daily. 'The House,' as it's affectionately called, is a beautiful 6,000 square-foot timber-frame building set apart for prayer. It's vision is to restore hope and bring life back to the people of God.

It was such a humbling and intimidating experience to step into the position of Director at the House and say, *'I will give myself to healing. I will pray for the sick, broken, and beaten-down people. I will lay down my life.'* Thankfully, I had a powerful, loving husband who supported me in this new and challenging role.

Since that day, my life has opened up in a
whole new way. The words that were spoken
over me at sixteen were coming to fruition before
my eyes. I wasn't going to a third-world country
or any back alleys to pray for others. God was
handing me the opportunity to pray in a beautiful
home specifically built for Him. It was time to
give myself to healing; healing of every kind —
emotional, physical, spiritual and relational. But
giving yourself to healing doesn't come without a
price.

Jesus paid a great price so He could pray
constantly for those around Him. We don't think
about all the times He was exhausted beyond our
comprehension. I know there were many
sleepless nights that we don't even know about.
Countless times He must have felt completely
drained from the exertion, but He continually
gave Himself to healing and to all the people
around Him. He kept giving. He kept praying.
He became the picture for all that would follow
after Him.

Do you think that anyone ever asked Jesus

how He was feeling? Did the crowds of people seem concerned for His strength? Many times we have prayed and asked Jesus to make us more like Him. Are you ready to begin that journey, or do you just want to receive the benefits and recognition of a life set apart?

Spending so much of my life in 'The House of Hope and Healing' has given me a *glimpse* of Jesus' world. For twelve years, I have been on call 24/7. Daily, I have prayed with guests on the phone or at The House. In the middle of the night, I have prayed with people calling the emergency line. Could you handle receiving hundreds of prayer requests in one week? How would you feel if people showed up at your house for prayer on Christmas morning? I've actually lived this way for over a decade.

I have prayed for countless people until I had no energy left; I have cried my eyes out for others until there were no more tears, and I have given away my 'me time' until I forgot the concept of it. We are living in a world that says, *'Hang on to your life. Take time for yourself. Remember your needs first.'* But Jesus said:

* * *

"For whoever is bent on saving his [temporal] life [his comfort and security here] shall lose it [eternal life]; and whoever loses his life [his comfort and security here] for My sake shall find it [life everlasting]."
(Matthew 16:25, AMP)

This is the formula for life! Every time I give my life away, life comes back to me. Every time I hold on to my life, I feel drained and without purpose. Find new ways to give your life away. Pray more! Give more! Worship more! Find a church that equips you and enables you to give your life away. You were created to give and to pour out!

In Luke 10:27, Jesus says:

"...You must love the Lord your God with all your heart, with all your soul, with all your strength, and with all your mind..." (NLT)

Love Him with *all* your heart, soul, strength, and mind. What does that look like? It is the picture of Jesus. I'm not even sure I have met anyone who has accomplished this fully. This scripture might take our whole lives to do, but God isn't concerned with perfection. He's looking for the forward movement as we desire to live out this scripture.

FAITH ALWAYS FINDS A WAY

In Mark 2, four men lowered a paralytic man through the roof of a house to Jesus, the Healer. When I think of their act of faith, I'm amazed by the tenacity and dedication they put into lowering the man to Jesus. What a miraculous story of faith! But, the story began much earlier than the moment the paralytic man came in contact with Jesus.

Everywhere He went, Jesus drew a crowd. And on that day, it was no exception.

"And Jesus, having returned to Capernaum, after some days it was rumored about that He was in the house [probably Peter's]. And so many people gathered together there that there was no longer room [for them], not even around the door; and He was discussing the Word." (Mark 2:1-2, AMP)

There was a great gathering of people making their way into the house. As the crowd rushed in to find their spot, the majority of the people had passed by the paralytic man. Surely there were others that rushed by his mat as they approached the house where Jesus was speaking. How many people didn't think to bring the man in contact with Jesus? Did everyone scramble to get his or her place in the house, neglecting to think of anyone else in need? Not everyone. There were four men who wrote history by their act of sacrifice and faith.

"Some men came, bringing to him a paralytic, carried by four of them. Since they could not get him to Jesus because of the crowd, they made an opening in the roof above Jesus and, after digging through it, lowered the mat the paralyzed man was lying on. When Jesus saw their faith, he said to the paralytic, 'Son, your sins are forgiven.' " (Mark 2:3-5, NIV)

Not only did they carry him, they broke through the roof of a house carefully lowering him to the One who could heal him. This wasn't a group of men who would say, *'I'll remember you in my prayers'* or *'Everything happens for a reason.'*

This was a group who took action! These men gave themselves to the healing of the helpless, paralytic man.

This account only mentions these four men of faith and the religious leaders who were speaking against Jesus in their hearts. No one else in the house was a focus. *Jesus saw faith in one group and unbelief in the other. When you respond in faith, you will see healing! When you respond in unbelief, you will be forgotten and rebuked.* These four men were heroes. They were going to do anything to get this man in contact with Jesus! This combination of action and faith was the catalyst needed for Jesus to heal the man.

As we read this account, we so easily assume that we're part of the faithful group of four that brought the man to Jesus, not realizing how many times we've rushed to get the best seats, leaving those in need behind. Would we have been the crowd that passed by the man? And later, how many people saw the miracle and wished they had been a part of that moment?

This crowd didn't make room for healing. Why did the paralytic man not make it to Jesus through the house door? Initially, it was because of the crowd! First, many weren't willing to pick him up. Then, when someone finally did, it was too late to get a place close to Jesus. Imagine how disheartening it must've been for the men when they arrived at the doorway and saw that no one was willing to budge for them.

But these four men didn't give up. Their faith found a way! They figured out how to get him on the roof, make an opening, and build a means to lower him down. This took great time and energy! They worked for this man. As they dug through the roof, it would've been a dirty, sweaty job. And remember, they didn't look for the chance to get near Jesus once the roof was open, but gave up *their* opportunity for someone else. That is the picture of prayer. They endured setbacks and overcame obstacles. It was a life-changing moment when four men took hold of God's will and didn't let it go until it came to pass. It's time to apprehend the will of God!

WHAT IS GOD'S WILL?

The phrase, *'If it be Thy will'* should be

banned from every believer's vocabulary. Jesus never prayed this phrase because He knew His Father. Religion has taught us to say this and other phrases like *Everything happens for a reason.* These statements become predominant in conversation when no one knows God's true will.

In Matthew 5:34, according to *The Message*, it says:

"You only make things worse when you lay down a smoke screen of pious talk, saying, 'I'll pray for you,' and never doing it, or saying, 'God be with you,' and not meaning it. You don't make your words true by embellishing them with religious lace. In making your speech sound more religious, it becomes less true."

This verse is usually applied to making oaths, but the truth of this statement rings true even in the midst of casual Christian talk. These are not the words I would want someone to tell me in a time of crisis, nor would I want anyone to speak these words over those I loved and cared about.

Many times, I have shocked people by my

response when they say, '*Remember me in your prayers,*' and I tell them I won't. Why wait and see if I remember? We should pray right now! I find it very odd when people want someone to pray for them, but don't necessarily want to be there to hear it. I want the person to join with me, hearing words of hope and life as I speak to God on their behalf.

ASK HIS WILL

I John 5:14-15 says:

"*...this is the confidence (the assurance, the privilege of boldness) which we have in Him: [we are sure] that if we ask anything (make any request) according to His will (in agreement with His own plan), He listens to and hears us.*" *(AMP)*

As we ask according to His will, with assurance and boldness, He hears us. And what is His will? Anything that's in agreement with His plan. Our God wants to save, deliver, and heal! Sadly, many Christians believe that God is okay with sickness and death. Surely He is calling some people home, right? No! Sickness is an enemy. God gave His son to die for us, that we might *live!* Our God is not double-minded. He's not holding anything back from us in His Word. His desire is to make us well—spiritually, physically, emotionally; in every way!

"Sickness is an enemy that God gave His son to die for us, that we might LIVE!"

Luke 12:32 says:

"Do not be seized with alarm and struck with fear, little flock, for it is your Father's good pleasure to give you the Kingdom!" (AMP)

You don't have to be caught off guard when you know your Father's will. He doesn't operate like an absent father. He wants to be fully immersed in your life! Luke says that it is God's pleasure to give us the Kingdom, which is *all* of its blessings, benefits, and wholeness. He's ready to release the Kingdom to us if and when we ask. *It's time to realize that it isn't the Kingdom that's lacking; it's the asking! We have not because we ask not!*

NEGATIVE CATALYSTS

I have seen thousands of people, sick with various physical conditions, needing prayer. But, one of the most crippling things affecting them isn't always the diagnosis — it's the destructive power of statements made by their well-meaning friends and family. Many of these loved ones haven't taken hold of the life and truth of the Kingdom of God.

When you're sick, these sympathetic people come out of the woodwork with stories of explanation and *'relevance.'* They inform you that their Aunt Martha went through the exact same ailments and received the wrong treatment. *'Watch out for those doctors, 'cuz they nearly killed her!'* It's as if you're in third grade again and once a subject is brought up, everyone has a story to tell about it. Unfortunately, they're not the life-giving stories that you desperately need to hear when you're sick.

In most churches today, Christians have gotten to a place where the sickness and disease seem almost normal. Faith in healing, by fasting and prayer, is rarely taught; much less put into practice. Ask anyone who is sick. Sometimes sick people are asked what sins they have committed that contributed to their diagnosis. Others are told that they have no faith and that God is trying to teach them something. Do you know any earthly father willing to do that? *Imagine a father giving his child cancer because they were disrespectful. Or a mother giving her teenager diabetes because they didn't clean their room.* My heart is crushed at the thought.

Our God isn't the one making you sick. *People in Heaven are not sick, so we can clearly see that it's God's will that we also be free from sickness and disease.* It's time to break out of the molds that keep the people of God captive to the enemy's tactics. Healing is a forever-covenant promise. God does not waver; Jesus does not waver. *He knows the price He paid to bring healing to you.*

THE PLAYGROUND BULLY

Let me explain it another way: growing up in any school system today can be very challenging for some kids. Teasing, bullying, and harassment on the playground are common to the children who are considered less popular than the others.

As the bully scours the playground looking for a weak target, the other children turn away in fear, not wanting to get involved. To me, this is a picture of sickness that's prevalent in the world today. A bully called sickness and disease is strolling through churches, looking for anyone it can devour. It's out to destroy you. It can't be reasoned with, and it doesn't take a break from its plan of destruction.

As the church body tries not to get involved, many innocent people are being harassed and bullied. Without the right tools and faith in God, the church has had no answers, and turned a blind eye to the attack. Ultimately, many Christians have died because the church hasn't stood up with faith and fought. The response of the church as a whole, is not to counteract what sickness and disease have done. I look at the Lord fiercely fighting for healing and life, and then I look at the church and it *doesn't* match.

But it's time to fight back. What causes a bully to back down? The once tough and intimidating playground bully will run and whimper like a wounded animal once he's seen a unified force step up against him. When the children stand up to him together, everything changes. What would happen if the church, the body of Christ, did the same? Sickness and disease would begin to flee. Show me a church that has minimal sickness and I'll show you a church that is starting to stand together and fight!

CONFIDENT EXPECTATION

It's time to become a life catalyst. Begin saturating yourself with words of life and health. Surround yourself with the will of God. Choose now to become someone that has the Word of God, like a fire shut up in your bones, ready to pour out to those who are hurting! You are the one that can have confident expectation of healing, rescue, and restoration. Stand up to the bully and he will run home crying.

Become the friend that comes out of the

woodwork with stories of hope and restoration. You can't just pray and *know* that God can heal. The devil knows God can heal. *You must expect it!* Become the one who believes God when He says that His will is to heal all who are sick.

Meditate on scriptures you want to begin to believe. He hears when we ask according to His Word. His will is His Word. Read these words aloud — they are *His* Will:

"O Lord my God, I cried out to you for help and you RESTORED my health." (Psalms 30:2, NLT)

" 'For I know the plans I have for you,' declares the Lord, 'plans to PROSPER you and not to harm you, plans to give you HOPE and a FUTURE.' " (Jeremiah 29:11, NLT)

Our God has *plans* to prosper you! He has *plans* to give you hope and a future! He's not waiting for you to mess up so He can harm you. Begin to develop your relationship with Him, learn to fast and pray with power, and He will cause healing to flow through your life and hands!

Don't Read My Book

Many people go through life's hardships and say, *'Thank God that chapter of my life is over! I have closed it forever. I will never allow that to happen to me again.'* They may have experienced a divorce, a traumatic event, or death of a loved one; and believe they have closed that chapter of their life. Others are devastated by abuse or rejection. We all have a story written of our lives with chapters completed, and many not yet written. Everyone's life is a book; there are areas of our own book that we wouldn't want anyone to read *ever*, and other areas that are tattered and worn by constant use.

Countless believers learn how to keep the secretive areas of their lives safely tucked away. Fear, sadness and doubt are hidden away in chapters that never open. Many try to present themselves to the world as successful and problem-free, while living paralyzed behind closed doors. However, when the tangible presence of God comes near them in prayer, many pages of their book will fly open again. There are people who can't move to another chapter of their life because twenty years ago they were offended or rejected, and they are still bitterly, forcefully hanging on to that one page in their lives. It might be the page that is nearly ready to fall out of the book, as they constantly turn to it with their thoughts and emotions.

As people ask me for prayer and start talking about their situation, they do not even realize they are saying, *'Let me show you my book. It has such a beautiful cover and is bound with the most expensive leather. This is who I am. I need prayer, but only for this page! Don't you dare turn to any other area!'*

UNDER LOCK AND KEY

As you develop in prayer and fasting, you also learn to read people's lives. I listen to men, women and children talk about their prayer needs, but I might actually hear fear and rejection. Don't look only at what you see on the outside. Begin to believe that you can read their lives, their heartache, and bring rescue. Even if they sound like the most confident people alive, God could be showing you that they are in torment every night as they're afraid to go to bed.

How do I know it's possible to read someone's book? Jesus did. He told the Samaritan woman at the well exactly what she was dealing with. With great care, He spoke to her right where she was, even though a Jew speaking with a Samaritan was against the culture of their day. He gave His attention to her. One of the greatest attributes of Jesus was that He *looked*. He saw with eyes of great compassion and love. He showed her that she was living in her own private jail, seeking out men to fill a void, but instead, she could experience the living water of God. She experienced a drink from God as He gave her the chance to break free from her past. Reading people's books brings salvation to many. Not only did salvation come to her, but John 4:39-42 says:

* * *

*"Many of the Samaritans from that town believed in him because of the woman's testimony, 'He told me everything I ever did.' So when the Samaritans came to him, they urged him to stay with them, and he stayed two days. And because of his words **many** more became believers. They said to the woman, 'We no longer believe just because of what you said; now we have heard for ourselves, and we know that this man really is the Savior of the world.' " (NIV)*

"... one conversation with Jesus caused an entire town to open up and experience Him, bringing salvation to multitudes."

As you read their book, you are entering territory that has been under lock and key for many years. Some people's pages haven't been visited since they were written. Others have one or two pages they visit continually. More than likely, the woman at the well had not talked so candidly about her life with others. Most people of her day went to the wells in the cool of the morning or evening. Instead, she went to the well at the hottest time of the day, not looking to meet anyone, let alone talk about her life. But that one conversation with Jesus caused an entire town to open up and experience Jesus, bringing salvation to multitudes.

After one conversation with most Christians today, is your life changed? If you were to ask your friends and family what you are known for, what would they say? Are you known for complaining and speaking words of doubt? Or, are you known for your compassion, bringing life to those around you? Jesus was unforgettable. He could take one broken, ordinary life and make it remarkably significant with one conversation; He was monumental.

Do you believe you can speak to one person and change an entire town? You can! Freely God has given to you, and now it's time for you to freely give it away. If you don't share His freedom, you won't be able to keep it. Remember; in the Kingdom of God, one conversation can bring salvation to multitudes for many generations to come.

* * *

SETTING CAPTIVES FREE

Recently, I prayed for a woman who was one of the angriest people I had ever met. Even the other prayer ministers at 'The House of Hope and Healing' were telling me that they were so frightened by her, they actually didn't want to pray for her. When I asked who would be willing to join me in praying for her, they all pointed their fingers at each other. Finally, I took the bravest prayer minister into the room with me. As we began to pray, not only did the woman look as if she could punch someone, but she also began to get very restless. She was getting more and more uncomfortable because the presence of God was actually coming into the room. He was helping us read her book.

It didn't concern me that she was full of anger. I could see that rage was just a symptom of a life full of brokenness and heartache. Even though it was that page of anger that she quickly presented to everyone around her, that wasn't the page I was going to read that day. Instead, I began reading her pages of rejection, fear, and doubt. The Spirit of God was revealing who she truly was... someone who had lost all hope that God would want to do anything with her at all. To her, life was hollow and insignificant. She was just trying to get by without being noticed. Anger was a tool to push people away and it had worked until now.

"The Spirit of God was revealing who she truly was..."

As I began praying for her, she interrupted me, *'Oh wait, wait, wait, wait! I know what's wrong with me. I* **know** *what's wrong with me. I don't have any faith that God will do anything!'* She expected me to console her and focus my attention on the fact that God does want to do something in her life and that she must have faith in Him. Is that how I responded to her? No! Why? *Because it wasn't the right page!* I smiled and said, *'You know what? That's okay, because I have faith for you.'* She suddenly looked like a child who had been told *'no'* for the first time in her life. Once again, I didn't turn the page.

I began to pray again. Walls of fear and

disappointment were starting to crumble when, once again, she interrupted me... *'Oh, wait, wait, wait, I know what is wrong with me, I'm mad at God!'* Skillfully, she was telling me that I was reading the wrong part of the book. She knew her hidden pages were being exposed and the power of God was really there. She was expecting and *hoping* that I would be horrified and say, *'Mad at God? You can't be mad at God. How shocking! Let's pray about that right now!'* But that wasn't what I did. *I did not turn the page.* Once again, I smiled and said, *'That's okay! I want you to know that God is not mad at you. He loves and cares for you!'*

It was starting to become agonizingly clear to her that I did care. I was asking the Lord to help us see her and bring freedom to her life. Layers of despair were falling off her heart. In turn, she was strategically trying to redirect me to another page that was much more bearable, somewhere that she could still be in control of the situation and her emotions.

I began to pray once more. She realized that it was time to pull out the big guns as she knew I wasn't giving up on her. She needed to stop me in my tracks. After just seconds of praying, she interrupted me: *'Wait, wait, wait... I want to know something about you.'* She mustered up the angriest face she could and pointed a bony finger right in my face as she nearly shouted, *'What are **you** getting out of this anyway?'* I could have answered, *'A million dollars, that's what I'm getting! No wait, I enjoy being around angry people... No, that's not it either... After praying for 1,000 people, I win a new car!'* The answer is obviously none of these. But the true, heartfelt answer I gave her next caused her anger and fear to melt. I said, *'My desire as I pray for you, is that you wouldn't live another day with this broken heart. Jesus wants you! He's not mad at you. He has a plan for your life and wants to restore your future. Let me help you heal today and start a new chapter in your life with God.'*

As I've prayed over the years, I've watched first-hand the kindness and love of Jesus, reaching out to people. He has great compassion for you. This is described perfectly in Matthew 12:20; Jesus will not *'crush the weakest reed or put out a flickering candle. He will cause justice to be victorious.'* (NLT) God is not going to toss you aside. Nor will He blow out your smoldering flame. He wants to revive and rekindle your fire for Him!

"God wants you! He's not mad at you. He has a plan for your life and wants to restore your future."

There were no more interruptions. Walls of fear that had been built over many decades crumbled and fell. She cried tears that had been buried deep in her heart. This woman who had previously looked like she was going to knock me out was now hugging my neck. God closed a chapter of her life that had tormented her for years. She didn't have to hide behind anger anymore! The other prayer ministers were shocked at how her countenance had changed. Light filled her face and she had become a completely new woman!

It's time for all of us to become like Jesus and speak healing into the people that think their lives are over. Jesus prayed throughout His life. It was a continuous, steadfast and intense spiritual struggle. In prayer, he did not give up. *A pat on the back, a pot roast dinner, or a quick 'be blessed' prayer is not going to cut it.* Require more of yourself in prayer. Pray like you would want someone to pray and fight for you. Step out of your comfort zone and start bringing people closer to God. *It's time for you to read their books.*

THE FREEDOM OF
VULNERABILITY

Every relationship has its ups and downs.
Arguments and misunderstandings easily spring
up as we neglect protecting the unity and
relationship we have with our spouses. But even
in the midst of the most intense disagreement,
everything can change in an instant if they
became open and vulnerable. Ask anyone who
has a successful marriage, *'What does it take to keep
a happy relationship?'* They might tell you to love
unconditionally or to learn to let the little things
go, but essentially they are saying, *'Be vulnerable.'*
They might've had the worst attitude and said
things they'd both later regret, but if they'd reach
out to one another with their words, grab the
other's hand in love, or express sorrow for the

division they'd created, their marriage would turn around. Why? Vulnerability.

Fifteen years ago, I married a very passionate, dynamic man named John. Combine that with an equally passionate, fiery wife... me. I remember in our early years of marriage, he was much better at being vulnerable than I was. As a disagreement would intensify, he would reach out to me and say, *'You matter more to me than this argument. We need to protect us. It isn't worth it to fight.'* He was opening himself up to me with great vulnerability and changed the course of our marriage each time he did.

Like the covenant relationship of marriage, godly relationships will only work if you are open and vulnerable. Think of how God feels in many relationships. He created you and His love for you is endless. He desires to give you every good thing. But He can't do anything for you if you won't be vulnerable and open.

Imagine a love-struck husband who is crazy about his wife. He spends the day thinking of his beautiful bride and planning ways to take care of her. The husband brings home her favorite food, buys her flowers and surprises her with a gift. He has set up a wonderful evening, and can't wait to see her walk through the door! Now, imagine the wife coming home and ignoring it all. She doesn't eat the food, doesn't notice the flowers and refuses the gift box. She hides herself away as she doesn't feel worthy to receive his love. She is more acclimated with division and isolation, than her husbands great love for her.

"God can't do anything for you if you won't be vulnerable and open."

I've seen thousands and thousands of broken and scared Christians asking for prayer, unable to speak to God. They believe they are not good enough to pray at all. Some are angry and unwilling to take another step. That is when it's time to pray and help them open up and become vulnerable.

THE POWER OF A 4" X 6" CARD

One day, I saw a woman proudly carrying

a 4"x 6" card as she came up to me for prayer. On it, she had written everything that was wrong with her. It was completely full, and there was not one white space left. I spoke about this woman at a conference and thought it would be a great idea to fill up a 4"x 6" card just like she had. Wrong. It took *forever*! After the first ten things that I could remember from her card, my mind went completely blank. I had to start making things up to fill that card out: skin dryness, eyebrow pain, toe fungus and so on. Honestly, I don't know how she did it! It was making me dizzy just looking at it.

As I began talking to her about her prayer needs, she forcefully clenched her card and said, *'Here; I have written down everything that is wrong with me.'* It was so surreal that all her problems, health issues and concerns were written out meticulously on the card in *very* tiny handwriting. As she handed me the card, I could feel the power that she had placed in it.

She was eager to see me read all that she had written, but instead I took one quick glance at it and said, *'It seems like there are a lot of things going on in your body, but God is going to heal you today! We are going to pray for you and watch these problems disappear. You are going to be so glad we prayed!'* These were not the words she wanted to hear. She said, *'Oh no, you have to **read** it. How will you know what to pray?'* Clearly she had not read my chapter 'Don't Read My Book.' Then, I said with great compassion, *'God already knows everything that is going on in your body, so here is what we're going to do: we're going to pray, and you're going to be healed. And here's the exciting part… after we pray, I want you to tear this card up!'* She looked like she was going to pass out. I'm sure she was thinking I was crazy. She didn't want to hear that she was going to be healed, or that God knew everything she was going through. Her only focus was, *'I want you to tear this card up.' (Insert dramatic music here…)*

I trudged onward, despite her look of shock and horror, *'This is going to be wonderful. I am so excited to share in this moment with you! God is going to heal your body, mind and soul. You are going to leave here a changed woman!'* I was asking her to be vulnerable in tearing up the past, the pain, and the disease. Still, she was not hearing all of my

words. But that was okay. I didn't need a 4"x 6"
card. I had God helping me read her life story.

Then we began to pray. It was an intense
time with many tears as freedom came. All pain
left her body and her hope was restored! But as
the presence of God put life back into her and
healed her body, it was still not enough. There
was some unfinished business. I looked her in the
eye and said, '*Alright, **it's time.** I want you to take
your card and tear it up and, as you do, God is going
to break the power of all these things that have come
against you.*' Then I handed the card back to her so
she could become vulnerable with God.

As she held the card, she realized the
power it had over her life. She was even unable
to move for a few seconds, feeling the weight of
what she was about to do. Slowly but surely she
began to tear away. I can still hear the beautiful
sound of that thick paper ripping! With each rip,
sickness was losing its hold and her heart was
softening. She was taking back her life in God!
Soon there were little pieces of confetti flying
around the room. Once she started, she became
overjoyed… and free. Next thing you know, she

was dancing and jumping on top of those little shreds of her past! She was a changed woman!

"When she tore that card, she was tearing off the enemy's words and death sentence."

We made her open and vulnerable, but what would have happened if she had received powerful prayer, and *kept* that card? Would there have been the same results? Absolutely not. That 4" x 6" card was much more than paper. It had become like a tattoo covering her whole body. It wasn't visible to our eyes, but the enemy had taken each problem and diagnosis, and marked her with it. *When she tore that card, she was tearing off his death sentence.*

Some of you now realize that you have been carrying your own card. It is time to rip it up! I even challenge you to write out the things that have had a hold on your life. Pray powerfully over yourself, asking God to bring healing and rescue to you. *Sickness and depression doesn't survive in His presence, why should it survive in yours?* You aren't called to be vulnerable to destruction. You're called to become vulnerable to God. Once you do, you'll continue to help others tear up the cards that sealed their lives in darkness and bring them into His glorious light! But don't forget, tear up that card!

MYTHS OF PRAYER AND FASTING

Despite all my religious duties and attempts at fasting, over time I was running aimlessly on a spiritual treadmill, and hiding from God with guilt when I didn't meet the standards I'd created in my mind. Sadly, when I became a Christian, I was bombarded with ideas of how to serve God, but these ideas only caused me to become more locked up. By the time I had achieved all the religious prerequisites for 'good' prayer and fasting, I didn't even have the heart to be spiritual. Here are some myths that are common among the people of God but cause only division and heartache:

Myth #1 - If I don't pray early in the morning, it doesn't count. The earlier the better!

Define early. Does it only count if it's with the rising of the sun? Many times I have thought, *'If it's a good idea to get up early 7 a.m. and pray, how much better it would be if I get up at 5 a.m. and pray. Those extra hours make it count even more!'* How self-defeating it is that the earlier, more restrictive and inconvenient prayer time is, the more genuine it is considered to be. Yet, too many Christians believe this and fail every time!

I remember many nights when I'd set my alarm for some crazy morning hour, planning to spend quality time with God. I imagine it going something like this...

As the sun is peeking over the horizon, I pull the blankets a little tighter to ward off the crisp, cool morning air. The covers have just reached that perfect, cozy temperature. Peaceful dreams of clouds and puppies fill my thoughts as I fall deeper into a 'coma state' of sleep.

Out of nowhere, the alarm clock sounds, tearing my dream away, dragging my mind and body awake. Surely it isn't time to wake up and be spiritual! But remembering how I promised myself I would get up and spend time with God, guilt overrides my rest. I force my body out of bed, pulling along my comforter and pillow, making my way to another equally comfy area. I wrap my snuggly soft blankets around my body, dim the lights and lay down. I expect to spend some powerful time with God. Instead, within seconds, I succumb to the cozy warmth. Sleep wins again!

Although I enjoy mornings, I don't bound out of bed ready to face the day with prayer and fasting, but God bless those of you who do.

Many times the Bible talks about praying in the morning, but the Bible also speaks of prayers on your bed and prayers in the night. Essentially, we are called to pray at all times!

Morning Prayers:

*"But to You I cry, O Lord; and in the **morning** shall my prayer come to meet You." (Psalm 88:13, NIV)*

*"In the **morning** You hear my voice, O Lord; in the **morning** I prepare [a prayer, a sacrifice] for You and watch and wait [for You to speak to my heart]." (Psalm 5:3, AMP)*

As I wake up, I am with God, speaking to Him. I live a life of prayer! But what happens to those poor people who work a night shift and cannot pray early in the morning as they sleep? Thank goodness the Bible speaks of night prayers, too.

Night Prayers:

*"... Jesus went out to a mountainside to pray, and spent the **night** praying to God." (Luke 6:2, NIV)*

*"... I remember You upon my bed and meditate on You in the **night** watches." (Psalm 63:6, AMP)*

Faithful Prayers:

*"Be joyful in hope, patient in affliction, **faithful** in prayer." (Romans 12:12, NIV)*

I have learned to pray whenever possible. Pray at all times for all things. Know this: the time of day you pray isn't indicative of who you are in God; your relationship with Him as you pray is.

* * *

Myth #2 - If I don't pray first thing when I wake up, it doesn't count.

I must admit, the first thing I think most mornings is, *'It's morning already?'* My thoughts aren't always filled with prayers and thanksgiving to God. Some of you shouldn't even think until you've had your morning cup of coffee.

A good friend of mine, Jessica, told me that her Sunday School teacher had taught her childhood class that if their first thoughts in the morning were not about God, then they were going to hell. What a devastating statement! Jessica struggled with that deceptive word for many years of her life, as each morning she woke up with dread, knowing she didn't think of God first. After years of torment, feeling like she wasn't capable of serving God, she turned to partying and seeking a man. She even said to herself, *'I'm going to hell anyway, I'm not cut out for this.'* Jessica longed to be close to God, but needed something to numb the pain caused by one statement that divided her from God.

No one should be taught that God is only good to those who think of Him first thing in the morning. Actually, the Bible says in Lamentations 3:22-23:

"It is because of the Lord's mercy and loving-kindness that we are not consumed, because His [tender] compassions fail not. They are new every morning; great and abundant is Your stability and faithfulness." (AMP)

"By the time I had achieved all the religious prerequisites for 'good' prayer and fasting, I didn't have the heart to even be spiritual."

No earthly father would reject his children because they didn't think only of him upon waking up. Every father is happy that his children want to spend time with him throughout the day. Thankfully, Jessica found freedom in God as she was filled with the Holy Spirit. She realized God wasn't asking her to live perfectly, remembering Him first thing every single day.

How is it that we make our God so strict and demanding? If any friend or significant other required you to think of them first thing in the morning every day, you might consider getting a restraining order! *Demands and requirements don't draw you closer to anyone.* God isn't asking for a morning roll call of perfection to prove your love. The *truth is* that God's mercies are new every single morning, and His loving-kindness is beyond our comprehension.

Myth #3 - My prayers won't change people's lives.

In Acts 3:1-8, one simple prayer changed a man's life forever.

"Peter and John went to the Temple one afternoon to take part in the three o'clock prayer service. As they approached the Temple, a man lame from birth was being carried in. Each day he was put beside the Temple gate, the one called the Beautiful Gate, so he could beg from the people going into the Temple.

When he saw Peter and John about to enter, he asked them for some money. Peter and John looked at him intently, and Peter said, 'Look at us!' The lame man looked at them eagerly, expecting some money. But Peter said, "I don't have any silver or gold for you. But I'll give you what I have. In the name of Jesus Christ the Nazarene, get up and walk!

Then Peter took the lame man by the right hand and helped him up. And as he did, the man's feet and ankles were instantly healed and strengthened. He jumped up, stood on his feet, and began to walk! Then, walking, leaping, and praising God, he went into the Temple with them." (NIV)

How many people passed by this crippled man with nothing to offer except a judgemental glance or some coins? Even though he was positioned right by the temple of God daily, he wasn't able to walk into the presence of God. No one came to help him beyond placing him in position to beg for money. There could've been people thinking the same myth you do... *"What difference can my prayers make?"* as they walked by.

In James 5:16(b) it says: *"The earnest (heartfelt, continued) prayer of a righteous man makes tremendous power available [dynamic in its working]." (AMP)* James doesn't say, *'The prayers of a perfect person make tremendous power'...* or *'Only Bible scholars who graduated with their Master's in Bible Theology can pray with power.'* Instead, it says that earnest, heartfelt prayers will reach the heart of God. And when God hears these prayers, He responds to His children. Every father does. And nothing breaks a father's heart more than not hearing from his sons and daughters.

Without prayer, we limit God and those we walk by every day pay the price. Just ask the man on the mat who encountered Peter and John. He needed their earnest, heartfelt prayers! This way of life isn't just for Peter and John. Your prayers can change lives! Step out in faith and believe that people will get better when you pray. You can bring them in contact with the living God and see results!

Myth #4 - Fasting is not my responsibility.

The ministry of prayer and fasting is given to the church as a whole, yet I know many Christians believe this lie. Peter 2:9 says:

* * *

"... you are a chosen people. You are a kingdom of priests, God's holy nation, his very own possession. This is so you can show others the goodness of God, for he called you out of the darkness into his wonderful light." (NIV)

We are chosen to pray. As a Christian, you have been called out of darkness into His wonderful light. Why? To bring others out as well by prayer! You might not feel like a kingdom of priests or a holy nation, but what can change that? Prayer!

I've had many people ask me how I pray like I do, and want me to tell some great secret of my ability. I know I personally searched for those secrets in books and articles, before I realized the answer. I know I have a few of you on the edge of your seat, waiting for the formula. There is no formula. It's one simple word. *Practice.* How do I develop my prayer life? *Practice.* If I want to be a pianist or a chef, what do I need to do? *Practice.* How does a doctor become a great surgeon? Years and years of school and residency cause him to *practice* medicine. Would you allow a surgeon to cut open your body if he hadn't gone to medical school? No! Yet, many Christians believe that we should be able to pray like Peter and John after saying the Sinner's Prayer. We might even get upset with God that we aren't able to pray with the same power as those who have been practicing it for years. Stop comparing yourself with others. I have a word for you... *practice.*

Myth #5 - If I don't pray at least one hour straight, it doesn't count.

I would like to strongly speak with the person that first listened to this lie. I remember when early in my relationship with God, I would try to pray for an hour. I was really proud of myself for about a minute. That's right, I was an excellent one-minute prayer warrior! After that, I would sputter out and wonder if I was even a Christian. I would even get one of those old kitchen timers with a chicken on top, and set it in anticipation of my great successful prayer time, only wanting to smash it against the wall when I failed. I feel bad for the poor people who pray for fifty-five minutes and then get pulled away suddenly for an emergency! Sadly, some believe all those prayers are wasted.

Instead, the Word says:

"Pray at all times and on every occasion in the power of the Holy Spirit. Stay alert and be persistent in your prayers for all Christians everywhere." (Ephesians 6:18, NLT)

Again, demands and requirements don't draw you closer to God. He takes joy in communicating with you throughout your day. Prayer is about relationship; don't limit God to a tiny, penciled-in appointment on your calendar.

Myth #6 - I can't fast and pray with power; I wasn't raised like that.

It is the Holy Spirit that empowers us to pray. He doesn't care how you were raised, or your denominational preferences. He enables a level of prayer in which *all* believers can function as the Holy Spirit enables them to do so. The church has many denominations and beliefs, but there is only one Holy Spirit. He doesn't cater to your church or the way you grew up.

"May the God of your hope so fill you with all joy and peace in believing [through the experience of your faith] that by the power of the Holy Spirit you may abound and be overflowing (bubbling over) with hope."
(Romans 15:13 AMP)

The deeper you hunger to see God and His answers, the deeper you fight to see God move. He will enable and fill you with the Holy Spirit, as long as you are willing.

Myth #7 - I must read about God in the Bible before I am able to pray to Him.

Should every believer be reading his or her Bible everyday? Yes! But it should not be a prerequisite to whether you can talk to God. Many Christians won't talk to God out of their lack of Bible study. Guilt wins. God is waiting for the chance to talk with His children; and we are concerned that we haven't read our Psalms, Proverbs, Old and New Testament reading plan for the day.

If you already talk to yourself throughout

the day, turn that conversation to the Lord. If you want a relationship with Him, be vulnerable with Him. It is a choice to open your heart to Him. As you pray, you can believe His promise: *"Draw near to God, and He will draw near to you."* (James 4:8, NKJV)

To understand it fuller, think of these myths operating in a covenantal marriage relationship. Would a wife or husband ever say, *'I can't spend time with you unless it is a full complete hour. Fifty minutes just wouldn't count.'* Or, *'Sweetie, I love you, but if I can't talk to you the very first thing in the morning, then let's not talk at all the rest of the day… it's just ruined for me.'* Imagine if a wife brought out her kitchen timer whenever the couple sat down to talk. Prayer is a relationship with the Father. *Without a direct relationship, it becomes a performance that no one wants to join.*

As you have read the previous myths, my prayer is that you become free from every limitation and obstacle, and begin to pray the Word of God boldly. Fuse yourself with His Word! Invest in the eternal, and you will see biblical results in your prayers.

PHYSICAL AND SPIRITUAL RESPONSE

The science behind fasting is simple. After starting a fast, many systems of the body get some greatly needed rest. Within the first few hours, your stomach stops its work and your liver gets a chance to recover. In a world where we're encouraged to eat five to six times a day, most people never give their digestive systems a break and time to detoxify.

As your stomach shuts down, extra glucose (sugar) is used for energy. Once that's gone, your blood starts to search throughout your body for dead, diseased and toxic cells. When found, these cells are consumed for energy. Instead of the energy being used to digest food, it's now available to heal your body. Your blood goes straight to the sickness within you and utilizes it, cleaning you of any toxic material. Fasting truly is such a beautiful picture of the body healing from the inside out. Biblical fasting is not starvation. As you fast, you consume stored energy or fat. Most people should have no concerns of ever starving themselves, as many of us have an abundance of *stored energy.* Yes, I did just call most of us fat.

I endorse people starting with short-term fasting rather than long-term. I've watched hundreds of people embark on their fasting journeys, proclaiming how the three day, twenty-one day or forty day fast was going to change their lives forever. With great zeal, they've posted it online for all their friends and family to see. Within days, their enthusiasm was gone and many abandoned the call of fasting completely. I urge you… no, I *implore* you, to start slowly. I highly encourage my students and others to start with fasting just one meal. Yes, one meal. *Not forty days to be more like Jesus.* Fasting isn't about quantity; it's about quality. I'm not impressed by your numbers. The consecutive days you fast mean nothing to me. *I'm impressed by your relationship with the Lord, the One Who activates your prayers and fasting.*

THE HEART IS WHERE IT BEGINS

Recently, my husband, John, and I were teaching a class on relationship with God. We asked the pre-teen students to describe God; to open their hearts and tell us about Him. While many stumbled over their words, John turned to me suddenly and asked me how I would describe him, my husband. I easily talked of my feelings of love, and of his great heart and humor, describing qualities that I knew without thinking. Tears came to my eyes as I spoke with great love.

Then, John asked me to describe my God. Instantly, my adoration for Him rolled off my tongue. My words were full of love and devotion. Tears rolled down my face as I described Him. As I spoke, my heart melted like wax toward Jesus. That kind of relationship makes it easy to fast effectively. If you can't talk about God, the One you are praying to with great love, how will you win the battle of fasting for Him and His people?

Fasting is a matter of the heart, not a matter of the stomach. We've had it backwards far too long. When you research fasting, and find much more about the flesh and the hardships you'll experience, rather than your spirit and the benefits you'll gain, something is drastically wrong.

"Fasting is a matter of the heart, not a matter of the stomach."

Fasting speaks from your heart. There might only be inches between your stomach and your heart, but in the spiritual realm it's larger than the Grand Canyon. I don't fast with my stomach in mind. I fast with my heart and the Spirit of God. Find out who He really is, and fasting will start to come naturally. Matthew 6:16-18 says:

"... whenever you are fasting, do not look gloomy and sour and dreary like the hypocrites, for they put on a dismal countenance, that their fasting may be apparent to and seen by men. Truly I say to you, they have their reward in full already.But when you fast, perfume your head and wash your face, so that your

fasting may not be noticed, obvious by men but by your Father, Who sees in secret; and your Father, Who sees in secret, will reward you in the open." (AMP)

Whenever I would read this passage in my early relationship with God, I would do my best not to look pained or to attract attention from others as I fasted. Most times, I wouldn't tell anyone I was fasting because I believed I would lose my reward. Thanksgiving wasn't the only time I pushed food around my plate in an effort to keep my fasting a secret, but I wasn't applying this scripture correctly. In this passage, Jesus was speaking to people who would purposefully look dreary so others would know they were fasting. They put on a spectacle and wanted the attention of men, not of God.

The real gem of this scripture is at the end of verse 18. *"Your Father, who sees (you) in secret, will reward you in the open."* Our God sees all and what He sees in the secret will be brought out into the light. What kind of fasting and prayer causes God to reward us out in the open? If someone tells you they fast, and you don't see the rewards of it in their life, they aren't connecting to God when they fast. Biblical fasting must be infused with prayer and the Word of God. Without it, you are just cutting out food. Anyone can do that, but few can fast and pray, seeing God bring rescue, healing and salvation to those they love. What does it look like to fast in such a way that God notices? That's the kind of fasting I want to do. Why keep fasting without results?

Physically, as I fast and pray, my blood is going after the dying, diseased and toxic cells throughout my body and using them for energy. But this is also true of the Spirit! Spiritually, my prayers while fasting are forcefully going after the dying, diseased and toxic people and situations in my life. My prayers are doing something much more than what they could've done without fasting. This kind of fasting adds sticks of dynamite to a flame! The word *dynamite* means something that has the potential to generate extreme reactions or to have devastating repercussions. Fasting empowers! Fasting propels and advances! When it's done through a relationship with God and a heart for people, fasting becomes an accelerated opportunity with extreme reactions!

My wonderful friend, Joanie, was learning
about how to fast and pray with power in one of
my classes. I encouraged her to fast only one
meal, devoting that time to God in prayer. She
excitedly described to me that one evening, she
made sure her kids were set with pizza and told
them she was going to her bedroom to pray. She
began to search her Bible for a specific chapter on
Esther and couldn't find it. As she started to get
frustrated, she remembered how I had taught her
that her focus needed to be on God. Joanie said:

*'So I stopped searching and just started writing
in my journal... I wrote and wrote and wrote to God; I
was so focused on Him and nothing else, that time flew
by and it didn't matter. I was crying and laughing
with God, experiencing God like I've never felt before. I
felt like I could conquer the world and anything was
possible!'*

Later, she came out of her bedroom and
had a bite of pizza with her children.
Immediately, guilt wanted to wash over her. Did
she just ruin the fast? Should she have waited
until breakfast to make the fast official? No!

Fasting is not about food. And eating does not end a spiritual fast. Your spirit and heart in relationship with God should determine the end of a fast. After spending time with God, she joined her children knowing her fast was empowered and activated by her relationship with Him, and not by the perfect number of hours she prayed.

"Eating doesn't end a spiritual fast."

Joanie's fasting experience makes me so happy. Who can describe their fasting moments with God like this? Not many. But that doesn't have to be the case for you anymore. You *can* fast with great joy and know that anything is possible!

FASTING PITFALLS

While researching fasting, I found abundant information explaining how to start a fast, or, in my words, how I would *never* start a fast. The following list was provided as a step-by-step process on multiple websites. Let's take a moment to break it down, showing why this doesn't work.

1. **Decide your objective.** This starts off okay. You do need an idea of why you're fasting. But, hopefully you have a developed relationship with God first.

2. **Prepare yourself spiritually by making a list of all your sins.** Um... *all* my sins? Thankfully, I didn't read this early in my walk with God. With great remorse and self-condemnation, I would've written

every sin that I had committed since birth, and wracked my brain for anything that I might've forgotten. Heck, I probably wouldn't get past this step to start the fast. And if I did, what good could I do with my guilt-ridden focus?

3. **Confess every sin the Holy Spirit brings to your mind.** Oh... my... goodness! This would be another train wreck for me. My mind would search frantically through my memories to make sure there wasn't a sin I was forgetting. What happens if I remember one mid-fast? Do I start over with step number one?

4. **Seek forgiveness from others.** So... does that mean every person that I've sinned against? Ever? Wait—I do have that list I just made of all my sins. Again, this step would take a tremendous amount of time. I find it hard to believe that Esther or Moses did these last two steps when they started a fast.

5. **Ask God to fill you with the Holy Spirit.** I'm certain I needed this step first. I know I could've used the Holy Spirit to help with my *massive* list of sins, confessions and forgiveness.

6. **Surrender your life fully to Jesus.** Wait. What? Who was I surrendered to before? Shouldn't I have done this way before now? Jesus could've helped me with all those lists!

7. **Meditate on the attributes of God.** It's always good to meditate on God, but this step almost seems thrown in. Honestly, everyone should already know many attributes of God before a fast because of their intimate relationship with Him.

8. **Do not rush into the fast.** *What does that mean?* How much time should I wait before starting? I don't recall that thought process being in the Bible. Esther couldn't say, *'I'm sorry, Mordecai, I need a few days to prepare before the fast. I'm sure you understand.'*

9. **Plan to rest.** Fasting will zap your strength. You won't want to run a marathon. But when planning a fast, I don't schedule my resting time. As Moses went up Mount Sinai, God didn't fly him up in a helicopter. God didn't put him up in a four-star hotel to rest either. Moses *climbed* it, twice!

10. **Eat raw fruit and vegetables for two days before starting.** I've read this on many websites and each time I do, it makes me laugh. I know myself. In my early walk with God, I'd likely end up eating a steak the night before the fast in 'preparation.' And, if I did eat fruits and veggies for two days before fasting, I'd call it complete—a two-day Daniel fast.

11. **Put yourself on a spiritual schedule by reading and meditating on God's Word, preferably on your knees.** I'm nearly speechless, but I must keep writing. This step started out so strong! I'm sure there are people that like to pray on their knees, but I'm not one of them. Unfortunately, I was so legalistic at one point, I would've

worn my knees out trying. *Remember, God's focus is not the position of your body, but the position of your heart!*

12. **End your fast gradually.** I couldn't agree more. But regrettably, I don't think I'd even make it to this step due to all the confession, forgiving and fleshly preparation before starting.

"Fasting, as we know it in most churches today, is starvation with great fleshly preparation and minimal spiritual relationship."

When we fast, is this the way the Lord wants us to prepare or are these steps a legalistic checklist? Do you feel closer to God after each step? No. *Fasting, as we know it in most churches today, is starvation with great fleshly preparation and minimal spiritual relationship.*

In Isaiah 58:3-7, the people speak to God, showing that they are only abstaining from food and looking for validation:

" 'We fast to show honor to you (God). Why don't you see us? We starve our bodies to show honor to you. Why don't you notice us?'

But God says, 'You do things to **please yourselves** on those special days of fasting. And you punish your servants, not your own bodies. You are hungry, but not for food. You are hungry for arguing and fighting, not for bread. You are hungry to hit people with your evil hands. This is not the way to fast if you want your prayers to be heard in heaven! **Do you think I want to see people punish their bodies on those days of fasting?** Do you think I want people to look sad and bow their heads like dead plants? Do you think I want people to wear mourning clothes and sit in ashes to show their sadness? That is what you do on your days of fasting. Do you think that is what the Lord wants?'
" (ERV)

The people of God are not fasting for Him. They're fasting to make themselves look better. They fast for prestige. They argue and fight amongst themselves while people are needing the church to truly fast and pray with biblical results.

In verses 8 and 9, God tells us:

*"I will tell you the kind of day I want — a day to set
people free. I want a day that you take the burdens off
others. I want a day when you set troubled people free
and you take the burdens from their shoulders. I want
you to share your food with the hungry. When you see
people who have no clothes, give them your clothes!
Don't hide from your relatives when they need
help." (AMP)*

**"True, God-given fasting is a picture of
walking up to prison gates, commanding
them to open and watching multitudes
of innocent prisoners walk
free."**

Many people have told me that they were
fasting, yet I could see they didn't care about the
people around them. It was evident they weren't
fasting for God. *True, God-given fasting is a picture
of walking up to prison gates, commanding them to
open and watching multitudes of innocent prisoners
walk free.* How many people have this result when

they pray and fast? Not many. Why? Because powerful fasting and prayer is *not* list-making, guilt-ridden confession and religious resting. It is time for you to open prison gates and see people be set free by your prayers and fasting!

WHERE DO YOU START?

True powerful prayer and fasting is an amazing force. It's an arsenal more powerful than a dozen atomic bombs. It strikes with such a tremendous power that it forces a breakthrough, and brings God's answers on the scene. Many modern-day Christians have *never* been taught how to fast with this kind of strength and authority, or even to expect real results. But I'm going to show you how to begin this kind of fast:

1.) **Start with a relationship and developed prayer life with God.** Have some maturity in your walk. Don't start a twenty-one day fast while still learning how to love God. Get to know the One you're praying to! Fasting is an intimate act of a believer who knows his or her God.

2.) **Partner with God.** Let God know you are appealing and joining with Him on behalf of yourself, others or a situation. Partnering with God is stepping into your rightful place as a joint heir as you begin to hear the heartbeat of God. Could anything be better than joining with the King of the Universe and His desires?

3.) **Make confident declarations!** Start to courageously declare who God is and what you believe He will do in your life! Begin to say phrases like: *'God, You are faithful! You are my healer! You plans for me are prosperity and health! You are my God!'* And then, believe your words! Prayer and fasting should be so full of faith and expectation, that it's just like turning the key in the ignition, and *knowing* your car will start.

4.) **Be willing to pay a price.** Realize that fasting will cost you and choose to volunteer. It will cost you time and energy. Fasting involves laying down your life and taking a risk. It is not for the faint of heart and it isn't supposed to be. God will sustain you and give you strength, but your efforts are needed.

When I look back on my life and realize how I'd made fasting and prayer a bondage, I yearn to see those chains broken off of others, who are doing the best with what they know, much like I was. I thought fasting was a deep ritual; that if I finally did it *the right way*, I could experience God. Instead, I was missing out on such a powerful opportunity.

Fasting is born out of true relationship as our hearts are united with God's heart, and we fight for His restored order of life. It's an ache and a passion for justice to prevail. God is searching for those who have stepped into this fight; who feel the urgency of the hour and are willing to be courageous enough to walk into the presence of the King.

To me, spiritual fasting is a gift—God is not taking food away from me. He isn't bearing down on me, showing me how many things I need to give up to have Him. I'm not giving up my life of enjoyment as I fast and pray. It's a gift to get so close to the heart of God that you don't want to eat. And, as He's giving me His heart, He's sharing with me His ache to see lives restored.

Fasting becomes a lifestyle of being so captivated by God and the need to see life restored, that there are times you just can't eat. *Spiritual fasting is a supernatural ache to see the salvation of the Lord come to the earth. It's a heart that won't take 'no' for an answer as you seek to bring back God's order of life for your family, friends, community and world.* My mind has been transformed in such a dramatic way that I now realize I don't *have* to fast, but I *get* to fast for Him.

"It's a gift, to get so close to the heart of God that you don't want to eat."

As I've broken free from the bondage of fasting, prayer has opened up a whole new level of relationship. I've realized it can become a way of life. I've prayed deeply and ached to see God heal in some of the most desperate times of my life and the lives of others. Fasting has caused me to develop a courage and tenacity that knocks down spiritual doors that were firmly shut. Food was not an issue. Hunger was not my focus. *My prayers went so deep that it felt like my stomach swallowed my heart.* Many times I've fasted and didn't even know it. Fasting is about the ache in your heart. If you have an ache for something, no one has to tell you not to eat.

Fasting will cost you. Many people already know it will cost them their three square meals and two snacks a day. The first thing that comes to mind for them is great sacrifice of what they won't get to put in their mouth. But fasting is far beyond this way of thinking. If food is your focus, then you are only operating on a baby level. If I took food out of the equation, what would make your fast different than any other day?

"My prayers went so deep that it felt like my stomach swallowed my heart."

Biblical fasting asks you, *'What are you willing to lay down to have the heart of God?'* Fasting is a heart seeking earnestly after God — seeking Him, not dinner. *If not eating during a fast is hard for you, then you're doing it wrong.*

As I have grown in God and understanding, fasting has become an overwhelming ache. It's an ache to see God's will on the earth today; to see healing and rescue come to those who are in great need. Ache, according to the dictionary, is an emotion experienced with painful or bittersweet intensity. When I think of *ache*, words like longing, craving, all-consuming, compelling and urgent come to mind.

Fasting that changes the world shouldn't be taken lightly! In order to fast and pray with power, there must be a fire in your belly for the things of God. Otherwise, there will only be the sound of your belly rumbling and growling for food. Fasting can save nations! It can change history! It will cost you, but the rewards are beyond imagination.

As you combine your prayers and fasting with the King of Kings, Creator of the Universe, brace yourself for a collision. You will see light and darkness collide and one will overcome.

When Esther sat at the table with King Xerxes and Haman, there was a collision in the spirit realm. God's angels declared war against the kingdom of darkness. Over Esther's table, angels were battling her enemies faster than human eyes could see. Esther's fast caused the heavens to be moved and war to break out. That's what happens when you fast and pray… you join God in a fight for His people!

"As you combine your prayers and fasting with the King of Kings, creator of the universe, you'd better brace yourself for a collision."

BENEFITS OF FASTING

In Isaiah 58:8-9, the benefits of fasting beautifully unfold:

"Then your salvation will come like the dawn, and your wounds will quickly heal. Your godliness will lead you forward, and the glory of the Lord will protect you from behind. Then when you call, the Lord will

answer. 'Yes, I am here,' he will quickly reply." (NLT)

Every morning we wake up, expecting the sun to rise, bringing new life. This is the picture of fasting! Darkness might be permeating every area of your life, but with the *activated power of God through fasting, light bursts forth!* Nothing can hide from His glorious brilliance! His salvation breaks through and our wounds are healed! Righteousness wins. Justice comes. God surrounds your steps and paves the way, bringing light to your path! While you fast, your enemy only sees God *surrounding* you with *His* righteousness, justice and glory!

"While you fast, your enemy only sees God surrounding you with His righteousness, justice and glory!"

But this happens only when we are fasting correctly. Our enemy isn't stupid. His goal is to make sure that Christians never fast with relationship, understanding or power. He laughs as many continue to fast with our flesh instead of the Spirit of God. And this has been happening since the beginning of time. I've said this before, but need to say it again:

Your enemy will tell you to do 'spiritual things' in a ploy to cause failure and ultimately separation from God. Sometimes we must realize that we have put God in a position where He looks much more like an abuser, instead of the Father He truly is.

I beg you to stop fasting without spiritual understanding. Develop an intimate relationship and then when you fast, God's light and salvation will burst into your life, His righteousness and glory will surround you and you will hear His voice say, **'Yes, I am here.'**

ONE PRAYER

One prayer can change everything. Period. Years ago, I heard a quote by theologian Walter Wink, *'History belongs to the intercessors.'* As I thought about those words and the power they contained, I realized that history had not always belonged to God's intercessors, those that stand in the gap as they fast and pray. History books are filled with devastation, famine and lost lives. Countless people and nations have lived through great carnage and mass murder. It's evident that, at times, history belonged to our enemy and not to the people of God. If history belonged to the Lord, the world would be like the Garden of Eden again.

Many times, *'C'est la vie'* and Murphy's Law, rather than the Word of God, rule

Christians' minds. Most people think that life will just work itself out, and I used to be one of those people. If it's meant to be, it will happen. God will make a way, right? *Wrong!* If I may so humbly add three words to Walter Wink's quote, I believe it can change the way you think about fasting and prayer: *'History belongs to the intercessors'... **or lack thereof.*** Life doesn't just go on. Intercession is not on the lips of every believer. There is a great deficit of prayer in the world today. But I want to help change that. Remember, every single day, your prayers are desperately needed so they can be lifted up to God. Join me in restoring history to God's intercessors!

BIBLICAL RESULTS

Moses changed the course of history with one prayer by imploring God to have mercy upon His people. Though destruction was imminent, Moses' prayers deflected God's wrath. Where would history have been without this prayer? Moses fasted and prayed, even when God had given up on the Israelites. Could you still pray and believe, even when God has had enough?

Esther's prayers saved an entire nation that would've otherwise been destroyed. Without her prayers and sacrifice, the book of Esther would've held the title of another name. You are like Esther. You have the choice to give your life for others or to keep it hidden. If you stay silent, you're agreeing with the enemy. You are called to be a voice of salvation.

"You have the choice to give your life for others or to keep it hidden."

Just like Esther, you were brought into the world for such a time as this. *You* are called to lay down your life and step into the battle. Don't let yourself be excused another day. If you want biblical results, you need to become like biblical people.

Daily, my heart burns in anger at the enemy who has come to bully the people of God, making them something they are not. They have listened to the voices of the enemy and stepped back from the fight. Each time they do, they die a little more. As they age, they're deadened to the voice of God. Many don't believe their prayers and fasting will change the world.

This is no time to hold your prayers back. If you won't speak, salvation will arise from somewhere else! You're not safe just because you're in a palace *or* a church. You must be able to walk down that corridor; to the very throne room of God. Again, your prayers will take you places that you weren't allowed to go. How unfortunate if you're a child of God and never walk into God's presence on behalf of yourself or others!

WHO CONDEMNS YOU?

In John 8, one of the most beautiful stories about Jesus unfolds. As Jesus was teaching, a woman who was caught in the act of adultery was thrown in front of Him by the religious leaders of His day. They made her stand in front of everyone as they began to question Jesus, asking what He wanted to do with her. They said she should be stoned to death according to Moses and the Law. They didn't care about the woman. They didn't care about justice. If they had, then

where was her lover? Their desire was to trap
Jesus. And that's what your enemy is continuing
to do to this day. He doesn't care about what
you've done; his goal is to bully and question our
God.

As they persisted with their questioning,
Jesus said:

*"Let him who is without sin among you be the first to
throw a stone at her. Then He bent down and went on
writing on the ground with His finger. They listened
to Him, and then they began going out, conscience-
stricken, one by one, from the oldest down to the last
one of them, till Jesus was left alone, with the woman
standing there before Him in the center of the court.
When Jesus raised Himself up, He said to her,
'Woman, where are your accusers? Has no man
condemned you?' She answered, 'No one, Lord!' And
Jesus said, 'I do not condemn you either. Go on your
way and from now on sin no more.' "* (John 8:7-11,
AMP)

It's time for all the voices to stop. Just like
this woman, we have sinned and deserve death.
But as Jesus speaks, all accusers begin to walk

away. Jesus is standing between you and your enemies. And He is speaking over you right now! He doesn't back down. His very presence shuts up the voices that speak against you.

Then, after all have walked away, Jesus, the One who has every right to condemn you, says, *'I do not condemn you either.'* You don't have to live in the realm with the accusers! God shows us His mercy and love. *Step away from sin and the enemy's accusations... and run to Jesus.*

YOU CAN BE GREAT IN GOD

Esther had a choice, and so do you. I wrote this poem as a response to every lie that has stopped people from walking into their destiny. It isn't life's obstacles that keep you from your future. It's your response. As you read these words, I pray that your eyes are opened and you're freed from every voice. No more agreeing with those that say you can't. May you know you *can* be great in God!

WHO TOLD YOU?

"Who told you you can't change the world?
Who told you you can't save a life?
Who told you it wouldn't matter anyway?
Who told you that you can't be great in God?

Who told you He doesn't keep His promises?
Who told you He is just the man upstairs?
Who told you you were a mistake?
Who told you that you can't be great in God?

Who told you you can't be powerful?
Who told you you are a disappointment?
Who told you you are destined to fail?
Who told you that you can't be great in God?

Who told you your dreams were foolish?
Who told you to give up?
Who told you you must live in shame?
Who told you that you can't be great in God?

Who told you you can't heal the sick?
Who told you you can't watch blind eyes open?
Who told you to hold back?
Who told you that you can't be great in God?

Who told you you can't pray and fast?
Who told you to wall in your heart?
Who told you you can't be like Esther?
Who told you that you can't be great in God?

Who told you He won't listen?
Who told you you weren't needed?
Who told you you can't hear His voice?
Who told you that you can't be great in God?"

May freedom come to you now in Jesus' name! I command all those accusing voices to stop! The Lord steps between you and your accusers as you turn to Him. Don't listen to voices that have an expiration date! Their time is up! You don't have to listen to those accusers anymore!

THE TRUE CATALYST

As you've read this book, you can see the progression of my lifelong search for a true catalyst. Through all the ups and downs, I have always wanted to come in contact with the true God. I thought that my purpose in life was to search and find God. I thought that by finding the prayer catalyst, the church catalyst or the healing catalyst I would be fulfilling the destiny I had in God. But this journey has brought me full circle.

The first true catalyst was Jesus Christ, and we are called to be His sons and daughters. We were born for such an hour as this! God is the one searching for the catalyst and we are it! *We are the catalysts to bring fulfillment of the Word and hope for the people of God.* We are the activators.

"The LORD said to me, 'You have seen correctly, for I am watching to see that my word is fulfilled.' "
(Jeremiah 1:12, NIV)

"We are the catalysts to bring fulfillment of the Word and hope for the people of God!"

We are the ones that cause the Word of God to advance at a *faster rate,* and we offer prayers that produce *significant change and action* in the Kingdom of God! Let me repeat the first words that you read in the beginning of my story:

'You have been called to be a prayer warrior. You are called to go to places that no one else will go; called to give in ways that no one else will give and called to pray in ways that others will not pray.

God wants to get you equipped. You need to practice. You might not be prepared for what is coming and you must begin to pray for people...

You are the catalyst to reach the nations. God is searching for men and women who will answer His call. Your prayers and fasting are the answer to a world in need. You must begin now.'

After reading my book, I would *love* to hear your personal stories and testimonies of fasting. Feel free to share your previous mistakes and your new successes in God! You can e-mail me at:

heather.eschenbaum@aim.com

Also Coming Soon: Fasting is Not About Food Workbook

CPSIA information can be obtained
at www.ICGtesting.com
Printed in the USA
FFOW05n2250260715